OLOGUB'S LITERARY CHILDREN:
Keys To A Symbolist's
Prose

Stanley J. Rabinowitz

Amherst College

1980

Slavica Publishers, Inc.
Columbus, Ohio

PG
3470
,T4
Z85

For a list of some other Slavica books, see the last pages of this book; for
complete catalog with prices and ordering information, write to:

Slavica Publishers, Inc.
P.O. Box 14388
Columbus, Ohio 43214

ISBN: 0-89357-069-9

Text set by Eleanor B. Sapp.

Printed in the United States of America.

TO MY PARENTS

CONTENTS

PREFACE

A former professor of mine, an expert on modern Russian poetry, once suggested that full-scale interpretations of such figures as Akhmatova, Mandelstam, Tsvetaeva, and Pasternak would be written only after some initial groundwork was laid. Each great poet, I recall him saying, creates his own view of the world, his private mythology. For the large elements of that system to be understood, not to mention placed in their larger context, the properties of individual works would have to be uncovered and many smaller, more modest investigations would need to be conducted. In the case of the four poets mentioned above, critical evaluation was at an early stage but the continual accumulation of ideas and theories about this writing could only hasten and facilitate the appearance of more complete studies.

These words are equally applicable to the study of Fedor Sologub and his literary legacy. A sizeable amount of modest investigations appeared before World War I, but since then critical evaluation of his work has proceeded at an exceedingly slow pace. However, the last several years have evidenced signs of renewed interest. His novels, *Bad Dreams* and *A Legend in Creation*, are readily available in English translation, taking their place beside his major prose work, *The Petty Demon*, which was translated in 1962. The Soviets issued a large anthology of his poetry as part of the "Bol'šaja Serija" project in 1975 and word has it that they will soon release a new edition of *The Petty Demon*. Sixteen of Sologub's stories were published in English in 1977, and at least one monograph and a dozen or so articles have been written on him since the mid-seventies.

Given the existence of these critical pieces and the increasing accessibility of Sologub's prose fiction to English-reading audiences, it has seemed appropriate at this stage to take a more comprehensive look at Sologub. The present study attempts to set forth some of the concerns, directions, and techniques which are reflected in Sologub's major prose while also making known, insofar as space will permit, the predominant critical opinions which have been expressed about this writing. As such, it anticipates further interest in this important Russian writer and suggests some of the areas where such interest might be directed.

Comprehensive analysis of Sologub's work is aggra-

vated by the general lack of attention which has been
paid to the period during which he wrote and the consequent disagreement over appropriate terminology to describe its different trends. It is commonly agreed that
the 1890s, when Sologub began his literary career, sig-
nalled a change in artistic values which was to have far-
reaching consequences in all spheres of creative endeavor
for at least thirty years. This overall trend of innova-
tion and flux is often called modernism. But this catch-
all term breaks down into smaller categories, at least
two of which, decadence and symbolism, apply to Sologub.
Generally speaking, the former represents the first stage
of the "new art" in Russia and it is basically characterized by an emphasis on the erotic, on volition, and also
by the presence of a pessimistic outlook which causes the
artist to withdraw totally inward and depend solely upon
the state of this inner world for his artistic matter.
Shortly after the turn of the century, decadence gave way
to symbolism, which focuses more upon inspiration and
upon religion, and betrays a more optimistic outlook
which encourages the artist to escape his "I"-centered
world to some higher form of reality, at times mystically
perceived. Ordinarily seen as an arch-decadent, Sologub
actually passed through each stage and his writing shows
traces of both. As further evidence of the plethora of
terms which exist to characterize this period, many in
Sologub's day labeled the initial stage of modernism
"neo-romantic" because they saw it as a rejection of
positivism and rationalism in favor of emotionality and
lyricism, with the related preference, at least initially,
for poetry over prose.

     While no one denies Sologub's firm standing in the
early phases of modernism (which continued on through the
twenties in Russia), his writing displays more traditional, less experimental elements than that of some fellow
prose writers of the period such as Bely and Remizov.
Indeed, Sologub has been called not only a decadent and a
symbolist, but a realist as well. This appelation is not
surprising if we realize that Sologub was born in 1863,
only three years after Chekhov and well before the great
novels of Tolstoy and Dostoevsky were completed. The
point is that Sologub is one of the oldest writers of the
"new" generation; his cast of mind was largely formed
while realism was still the predominant literary style
and his work reflects evidence of a considerable debt to
it.

In short, Sologub wrote during a period of great
flux whose definitive literary history has yet to be
written and whose different and often complex currents
await precise codification. With few exceptions, the
prose which Sologub produced during this time has been
unjustly neglected, as has his contribution to Russian
literature as a whole. Sologub's place in this great
literary tradition can be understood when the peculiar
flavor of his writing has been established. The present
study is meant as a first step in this direction, as an
intermediate stage between the modest investigations
which currently exist and the comprehensive study which
has yet to be undertaken.

Note on transliteration:

Anglicized versions of Russian names are used in the text. Scholarly transliteration is reserved for the footnotes and bibliography.

INTRODUCTION

"It is hard, indeed it is
totally impossible, to call a
writer in all of (Russian)
literature more original and
more enigmatic than Fedor
Sologub."

V. Bocjanovskij[1]

The name Fedor Sologub (pseudonym for F. K.
Teternikov, 1863-1927) began circulating widely in 1896
when three volumes of his work were published in separate
editions: *Poems (Stixi); Shadows: Stories and Verse
(Teni: Rasskazy i stixi)*; and the novel *Bad Dreams
(Tjaželye sny)*. Most of these pieces had appeared during
the past two years in the Petersburg journal, *The Northern Herald (Severnyj vestnik)*, which was sympathetic to
the newest currents in Russian literature.[2] Its editors,
L. Gurevič and A. Volynskij, had befriended the fledgling
writer in 1892, shortly after his return home to the capital from an eight-year position as a provincial high
school teacher, and in 1894 they gave him his literary
start. Sologub always considered that year as the official beginning of his career as a writer, but the mark
which he was to make upon contemporary letters became
evident only in 1896.[3] Ever since that time critics have
noted the uniqueness of this literary figure. His singular importance not only to the symbolist movement, in
which, to quote a recent Soviet publication, he was "one
of the seminal figures,"[4] but within the entire Russian
literary tradition has been attested to with convincing
frequency.

One of Sologub's constant admirers, Andrey Bely—
himself a giant of the period—insisted that "Tolstoj,
Puškin, Lermontov, Dostoevskij, Turgenev, Gogol', Fedor
Sologub were, are, and always will be our teachers."[4]
Evgeny Zamyatin, the author of the utopian novel *We*
(1921) and one of Sologub's fervent devotees, confidently
predicted that "cruel time will obliterate many, but
Sologub will remain in Russian literature."[5] Whether appreciated or not, Sologub's impact upon his contemporaries was enormous. Readers who did not necessarily understand or agree with his frequently elusive writings,
still reacted to him with intense curiosity. Perhaps it
was again Bely who most eloquently expressed what seemed

to be the rather widespread sense of admiration, fascination, and puzzlement regarding Sologub—even among those
who espoused negative sentiments about his work. He
wrote:

> In your works alongside an enormous talent there
> is a special note which gives an unanalyzable
> charm to [them]: it is an understatement to say
> that you infect the reader with a certain experi-
> ence; you hypnotize him, and thus your world-
> view penetrates the reader like contraband; I
> have experienced this witchcraft several times.
> Your position as a writer is exceedinly clear;
> one has to struggle with you. At least I have
> struggled with the "sorcery" of your words, but
> I, as a writer, pray to "other gods," not yours.[6]

Bely's statement is interesting more for his recognition
of the need to "struggle with" Sologub seriously than for
his acknowledgment of the curiously attractive power of
the actual prose.

Part of the struggle that many of Sologub's contemporaries faced was the difficulty in overcoming a bias
against Sologub-the-man, a bias which even occasionally
betrayed feelings of personal disgust. Almost all who
had dealings with the writer found him to be reclusive,
somber, and often morose; a cold, aloof, uncommunicative,
and inscrutable individual. "He was not loved, he was
considered to be an evil person; people feared him, and
even worse, they avoided him," writes Petr Ryss in his
sympathetic portrait of the writer. "He was cold in appearance, restrained, constantly sarcastic; his eyes had
an icy look and were half-closed, as if out of contempt—
F(edor) K(uzmič) frequently inspired hostility."[7] These
personality traits, coupled with Sologub's often obsessive pursuit of such decadent themes as death, corruption, and various sexual perversions, gave rise to an air
of controversy, if not a sense of derisiveness, which was
inevitably associated with his name.

Yet, even those who rejected Sologub's ideology and
private mythology as easily as they resisted the enchantment of his stylistic magic, often recognized in him a
writer of significant magnitude worthy of sustained critical attention. "Refuting or praising is not a very difficult matter; indeed it is of secondary importance.
More important is the need to understand. In any case,
Sologub is such a great and original artist that he

thoroughly deserves calm, dispassionate analysis even
from those who in essence do not accept him."[8]   So argued
with rare sobriety A. Dolinin in his own occasionally
critical analysis of Sologub's fiction, and many who
have followed him have shared this sentiment.   In his
long obituary of Sologub, Khodasevich invited his readers
to study him more exhaustively, claiming that eventually
"the work of Sologub will be pondered and studied deliberately and carefully.   By all the means available the
investigator will trace the thought concealed in Sologub's
multi-volumed collected works."[9]   A generation later,
Gleb Struve repeated Khodasevich's hope, insisting that
"at one point a genuine book will be written about
(Sologub)."[10]

Despite the periodic calls for more systematic and
thorough attention to Sologub, as well as the writer's
own insistence, with unquestionable reference to himself,
that "one can understand an author only when one studies
and studies all of him,"[11] relatively few commentaries
have appeared.   And most that have, have tended to concentrate on a single work at the expense of a fuller,
more chronological overview of Sologub's output.
Sologub's statement is obviously directed at those critics—and there were many in his day—who would arrive at
general conclusions about him on the basis of an often
limited and impulsive view of an isolated work.   Because
such criticism exists in abundance and because we are
now more soberly distanced from his writing, it seems
particularly appropriate to approach Sologub from a
broader perspective.   We would deal, if not with absolutely "all" of his works, then at least with representative samples which cover the major period of his long
career.

During this career Sologub succeeded in producing a
vast quantity of work.   His *Collected Works* alone, issued by the Sirin Publishing House in 1913-1914, fill
twenty volumes.   In addition to this there exist several
later volumes of poetry and prose written between 1915
and 1923, after which no new works were published.   There
is also a substantial amount of uncollected writing—
poems, stories, fairy tales—scattered in various news-
papers, journals, and almanacs of the day.   And this is
not to mention Sologub's unpublished materials which
Ivanov-Razumnik, who collected and deposited the writer's
archive in Leningrad's Institute of Russian Literature
(Pushkin House), claims consists of "hundreds of

unprinted poems, outstanding stories, plans for novels
and tales..."[12]   The sheer bulk of this output, the
product of more than thirty years of frenetic literary
activity, may itself be responsible for past reluctance
to approach Sologub on a large scale.

I, too, have been reluctant to assume here the considerable task of critically evaluating all of Sologub's
available writing. Nor is such an exercise essential,
if one chooses to look at Sologub primarily as a
decadent-symbolist writer. This was the period during
which he achieved his greatest notoriety and which ended
just about the time that his *Collected Works* were published by Sirin. Therefore it is these volumes—the
"standard Sologub"—whose contents were scrupulously ar-
ranged and whose publication was carefully supervised by
the author—upon which this inquiry is based. Secondly,
since Sologub deserves to be presented to the non-
Russian, as well as the Russian reader, it is his prose
which needs to be examined. Happily, much of this
prose—the three major novels and about two dozen of his
short stories—are available in English translation.
Approximately half of the volumes of Sologub's *Collected
Works* will be treated here; however since close thematic
ties exist between the writer's prose and his poetry and
drama this study should have implications for almost the
entire body of Sologub's pre-Revolutionary writing.

Even a casual reading of this impressive body of
writing reveals that among its many thematic components,
one in particular is repeated with remarkable constancy:
the theme of the child. A detailed investigation of this
theme leads to the complex metaphysical issues which pervade Sologub's work; it also provides a key to understanding his highly idiosyncratic vision of reality.
Vyacheslav Ivanov's famous contention that "the child is
the central point of (Dostoevsky's) doctrine concerning
the world and concerning man,"[13] is equally true of
Sologub. It might serve, if one were interested in the
problem, to initiate an extremely fruitful comparison of
the two writers, for no major Russian writer since
Dostoevsky has afforded the child such profound and
elaborate treatment as has Sologub. No detailed study
of Sologub can fail to note Dostoevsky's considerable
influence on the writer, and while a systematic treatment
of this legacy is not possible here, significant points
of coalescence will be mentioned whenever appropriate.[14]

Children appear in well over half of Sologub's

sixty-odd stories in his decadent-symbolist phase of
1894-1914, where they are, by and large, the author's
major focus of attention. Furthermore, in each novel of
this period, *Bad Dreams; The Petty Demon (Melkij bes,*
1905); the trilogy *A Legend in Creation (Tvorimaja
legenda,* 1907-1914); and *Sweeter Than Poison (Slašče
jada,* 1912) children play a crucial, if not a central,
role.

While on the subject of classifying Sologub's works
chronologically, it should be noted that rigid "periodi-
zation" of this writing is frequently difficult. But
Sologub's reputation as a major writer does coincide
with the rise and fall of symbolism as a literary movement in Russia, and this can be designated his first
period. Various subdivisions within Sologub's work do
exist, but as a study of his literary children illustrates, the structure and pattern of the writer's prose
during these twenty years are such that they invite cate-
gorization under one general heading. Indeed, the fact
that children are encountered so frequently here, while
they hardly appear in later creations, itself provides
sufficient impetus to consider the writing of this period as a single block. The years of World War I, 1914-
1918, may be seen to constitute Sologub's second phase,
which was marked largely by patriotic poems and stories,
most of which, to agree with one recent critic's evaluation, "makes embarrassing reading today."[15] Sologub's
third phase is represented by the post-Revolutionary
span of 1918-1927. During this time his poetic gifts
continued, but his talent as a prose writer slackened, as
Gleb Struve's comment about Sologub's one novel of this
period, *The Charmer of Snakes (Zaklinatel'nica zmej,*
1921) implies: "It is so bad that one might doubt that it
belongs to Sologub at all."[16] Whatever the merits or
shortcomings of Sologub's post-symbolist fiction may be,
these works do not fall into the purview of this study.

Sologub's use of children is especially interesting
from a structural point of view. While the child is almost invariably the hero in the stories in which he appears, this same character in Sologub's larger works
serves a consistently ancillary function; he is always
closely and vitally associated with the adult-hero who
is now at the center. (The exception here is *Sweeter
Than Poison* which, significantly, is an extension of an
earlier story, "Shanya and Zhenya," 1897, and lacks many
of the features of Sologub's other novels). Thus, in

terms of characterization, Sologub's major novels can be
seen as somewhat "bifocal." Login, the hero of *Bad
Dreams*, has strong ties to the young orphan, Lenya. Both
Peredonov and Ludmila have a peculiar relationship with
the school boy Sasha Pylnikov, the nature of which is
vital for understanding *The Petty Demon*. And Trirodov,
the protagonist of *A Legend in Creation*, has a son
Kirsha, as well as a colony of eerie quiet children
("tixie deti")—all of whom are central to the work's
plot and thematics. Even in Volume Two of the trilogy,
Queen Ortruda (Koroleva Ortruda), where Trirodov does
not appear at all, the "bifocal" quality is still maintained. The heroine, from whose name the title of the
book is derived, is paired with the young page, Astolf.
In Sologub's charming *Fairy Tales (Skazočki)* as well,
the child plays a major role; for the narrative viewpoint, which elsewhere in Sologub's prose has been conveyed largely from an adult perspective, is now entirely
the child's.

On the basis of the child's unique function in each
domain of Sologub's fiction—story, novel, and fairy
tale—one might establish what appears to be the writer's theory of genre which informs his prose. As we
shall see, there appears to be little doubt that a special relationship exists between the child's position in
a work's narrative structure, a position which differs
in each fictive mode, and the particular philosophical
stance which Sologub is currently assuming. It is as if
Sologub were using children for quite different purposes
depending upon where this character appears. Otherwise
stated, the very form or structure of Sologub's aesthetic
creations, especially as this form reflects the child's
function within it, is profoundly connected to his meta-
physics, to his attempt to fathom the meaning of life.
By examining Sologub's use of children in the various
literary modes which he employs, we can determine the
contours of the writer's transcendental vision. Such a
relationship between aesthetic form and philosophical
vision is best illustrated by a generic approach to
Sologub's fiction, and the arrangement of chapters here
proceeds along this assumption. However, it is a chronological consideration of his work which demonstrates
the evolution of Sologub's thinking, and I am mindful,
within and among individual chapters, of the child's
changing function through time. Sologub's literary
children are particularly compelling because, as an

obvious constant in his writing, they provide perhaps the
single most crucial barometer by which, to recall
Khodasevich, we can, "measure the thought" concealed in
his work.

The importance of children in Sologub's fiction can
be initially appreciated when one acknowledges the essential feature which characterizes the writer's art in general. This is a dissatisfaction with reality—both with
the external, physical reality of the author's environment as well as with the internal, spiritual world of his
own tortured psyche. A striking dualism runs throughout
all of Sologub's writing and is largely responsible for
the unusual tension and nagging uneasiness found there.
This dualism expresses itself as a continuing struggle
between a fierce hatred of the monotony and constraining
quality of man's earthly existençe and a resulting desire to transcend banality and escape to a higher state
of beauty and perfection. Despair over the drabness and
seeming hopelessness of the here-and-now, a mood which at
times predominates in Chekhov, alternates with occasional
hope for a miracle of salvation.

Sologub, we should recall, was as much "a son of the
eighties" as Chekhov; he was as much a product of the
weary decade of crushed hopes, lost faith, and intellectual stagnation as was the author of the early collections, *In the Twilight* (1887) and *Gloomy People* (1890).
The era of Tolstoy's *Confession* (1880), with its brutal
honesty in admitting the bankruptcy of previous spiritual
foundations; of Saltykov-Schedrin's *Forgotten Words*
(1889) and Turgenev's *Poetry in Prose* (1883), with their
ominous forecasts of the destruction of the world; and
of Chekhov's own early writings in which "the world is
collapsing"—"mir rušitsja"—(e.g., "The Reed Pipe,"
1887 and *The Wood Demon*, 1888)—all of this constitutes
a vivid reminder to Sologub of the terrifying void that
exists when a man's previous ideals collapse into nothingness.[17]   The dreariness and hopelessness conditioned
by this spiritual impasse represent the starting point
of Sologub's art; they create the emotional backdrop for
his major works. Yet Sologub's writing, which chronologically and spiritually extends well beyond the gloominess of the eighties and early nineties, contains newer
and more positive elements than the fiction of doom mentioned above. The fear of the end is countered by the
hope for perpetual beginning, which the child in
Sologub's work invariably signals. One of Sologub's

earliest poems relates precisely this idea.

Ja takže syn bol'nogo veka,
Dušoju slab i telom xil,
No stranno—veru v čeloveka
Ja prostodušno soxranil.

V bor'be uporno-bespoščadnoj
Sgoreli junye mečty,
Potoptany tolpoj zloradnoj
Nadežd vesennie cvety,

I dlitsja noč', černa, kak prežde,
Vsju zemlju mgloju polonja—
A vse že radostnyj nadežde
Est' mesto v serdce u menja!

I also am a son of this sick age,
Weak in soul and sickly in body,
But strangely my faith in man
Has innocently been preserved.

My youthful dreams have been consumed
In the stubborn and merciless battle,
The springtime flowers of hope
Have been trampled by the malicious crowd,

And the night continues, black, as before,
Conquering the whole world with gloom—
And yet there is in my heart
Still room for joyful hope.

(1892)

In a long and insightful commentary, Sologub's contemporary, the critic Aleksandr Gornfeld, ties the author
to the decadent movement, with its stress on individualism and eroticism and its attempt to obtain a "mystical
cognition of (the world) with the help of symbols."[18]
But it is Renato Poggioli's definition of this same current which captures the specific polarity of which we
have been speaking.

The cultural phenomenon which in modern literature takes the name of Decadence is possible
only when the vision of the impending catastrophe merges with the expectation that another

culture will be built on its ruin. That expectation may be only an illusion; yet the modern
idea of Decadence is based on such a dialectic.
An old, tired, and sophisticated society may at
least in part turn the very objects of its
fears into objects of hope.[19]

The title of Volynsky's influential book *The Struggle for
Idealism (Bor'ba za idealizm*, 1900) accurately describes
Sologub's own endeavor to believe in "the lofty and the
beautiful" (to use Kant's phrase which Dostoevsky also
found appealing), despite strong evidence to the contrary. That such a conflict assumed tragic heights in
Sologub is noted by Ivanov-Razumnik when he emphasizes
that although the writer sincerely sought a miracle, he
did not, and ultimately could not, believe in one.[20] To
phrase this Dostoevskian dilemma somewhat differently,
Sologub is seeking faith in a world in which faith is impossible, yet unavoidable.
    It is with the search for miracle, with the quest
for faith, that the child is most unarguably and consistently connected in Sologub's work. Among his poems,
which rarely mention children, Sologub openly revealed
this association:

    Ja verju v tvorjaščego Boga,
    V svjatye zavety nebes,
    I verju, čto javleno mnogo
    Bezumnomu miru čudes.

    I pervoe čudo na svete,
    Velikij istočnik utex—
    Blaženno-nevinnye deti,
    Ix sladkij i radostnyj smex.

    I believe in a creating God,
    In Heaven's divine precepts,
    I believe that many miracles
    Have been revealed to our senseless world.

    But the foremost miracle on earth,
    The greatest source of delight—
    Are blessedly innocent children,
    Their sweet and joyful laughter.

The child's recurrence throughout Sologub's literary

career, specifically during the years 1894-1914, attests
to the writer's continual need of a transcendent ideal.
Like those mystic or sickly characters—Sonya, Myshkin,
Marya Timofeevna, Kirilov, Zosima—who wander through
Dostoevsky's novels expounding visions of beauty,
Sologub's children appear again and again to express on
the part of the author a similar belief.

Sologub's use of the child as his master symbol of
this desired purity serves as an additional reason why
the symbolist movement has been called, and has a right
to be considered, neo-romantic. Just as romantic writers
a century before had used the child as a favorite device
to display their distaste for the preceding "Age of
Reason," so Sologub turned to this character to express
his dislike for the previous generation's positivist and
utilitarian excesses. Something beyond our materialist
world and better than sinful man must exist, and
Sologub's literary children illustrate the entire spectrum of emotions which the writer experiences as he
grapples with the ramifications of this conviction.

It seems appropriate here to mention that Sologub's
interest in children has a profoundly personal basis, and
one which goes beyond mere literary convenience. His
constant, indeed obsessive attention to children's, especially boys', pain and suffering, to their weakness and
impending loss of innocence, and to certain physical
features such as eyelashes, arms, and legs, has caused
many a reader to perceive in him deep psychological ab-
normalities. This may indeed be true. But interesting
as such a topic would be to explore, it is not in this
author's range of competence, nor is it the purpose of
this study, to investigate the relationship between
Sologub's personal life, such as it is known to us, and
his literary images and thematics.[21] The important point
to make is that Sologub's art, particularly as one recognizes the child's vital role in it, represents a perfect
blend of individual history and decadent literary tastes.
Sologub's literary children show that the writer's decadence was not simple posturing, as was the case in many
writers of lesser caliber during this time; rather it
stemmed from the deepest roots of his personality. Considering the peculiar nature of the artist's complex
psyche, Sologub wrote at an ideal period in Russia's literary history. Gornfeld sensed this when he claimed
that "it was not Fedor Sologub who came to decadence ...
but rather it was the literary movement which came to

him.... In Sologub Russian decadence found itself, its
genuine face, its justification."[22]

When studying the child as a purely literary phenomenon, one sees that his importance lies not only in his
embodiment of an ideal beauty and perfection. He is also
significant in his reflection of the different ways in
which this ideal can be attained. And here is where attention to these characters' chronological appearance in
Sologub's work comes into play. In the earliest phase of
of Sologub's decadent-symbolist period, roughly 1894-
1898, the child is generally connected to a Rousseau-
istically inspired state of pastoral innocence, with a
back-to-nature orientation. In the middle and darkest
segment of this period, 1899-1906, the child is often
associated with death. But death has positive connotations in Sologub insofar as it represents one of his
favorite means of escape from stultifying *poshlost*, a
term which connotes all that is vulgar, trivial, and
banal in life. And in his late works, written between
1907 and 1914, the child is tied to the notion of creative fantasy and its power to transform life, an idea
which represents a new optimism in Sologub. A major goal
of this study is to show how the child reflects a gradual
shift in Sologub from a position of extreme pessimism in
his early works to a considerably more optimistic posture
in his later writing. To demonstrate this shift is to
chart Sologub's movement from the dark nightmare of decadence to the brighter vision of symbolism.

For too long criticism has tended to view Sologub as
a singer of death, as a writer whose literary canvas is
uniformly morbid and dreary. "It goes without saying,"
argued the critic V. P. Kranixfeld, representing a majority viewpoint, "that morbid Sologub largely despises
life."[23] Even such well-qualified contemporary investi-
gators of the Russian modernist scene as Renato Poggioli
and Georgette Donchin concentrate exclusively on the
bleak side of Sologub's work. If anything, a study of
Sologub's children proves such treatment to be one-sided
and, ultimately, inadequate for a full appreciation of
the writer's scope. The child's varied and changing
function in Sologub's prose corroborates M. Dikman's recent observation that the lack of rigidly fixed stages
in Sologub's writing is no reason for "some people to be
led into denying any evolution ... at all."[24]

Such evolution, such fluctuating rhythm in Sologub's
fiction has largely eluded critics. Bely and Khodase-

vich, for example, although expressing great esteem for
Sologub's literary gifts, fail to acknowledge any meaningful development in his art—spiritual, metaphysical,
or formal. In fact, they have charged that such a lack
of development is a hallmark of Sologub's work.[25] But
the claim that Sologub's writing is monophonic in tone,
uniform in color and pattern, and static in emotion ignores the writer's complex moods and the corresponding
stylistic levels he uses to convey them. As one of the
oldest of the "new" writers who emerged in full force
soon after the turn of the century, Sologub passed
through all the stages which preceded and accompanied the
final establishment of symbolism as a respectable and
widely accepted literary movement. Sologub's fiction
contains within it a variety of different and often conflicting elements. Civic motifs comingle with decadent
themes, the everyday reality of the historical present
alternates with utopian dreams of the distant future. If
there is a certain amount of contradiction, not to mention eccentricity, here, then one would do well to heed
Chukovsky's evaluation: "However one relates to such a
strange body of work ... one thing is clear ... it has
been created by our age, it was dictated by it. In
(Sologub's) works, our age has been reflected as in a
mirror."[26]
    A study of the child, then, provides an effective
means by which to grasp the style and the vision of
Sologub's remarkable prose which is, as Chukovsky appre-
ciates, a mirror of the entire literary age to which the
writer belonged.

NOTES

[1]V. G. Bocjanovskij, "O Sologube, nedotykomke,
Gogole, groznom, i proč.," in A. N. Čebotarevskaja, ed.,
O Fedore Sologube: Kritika (St. Petersburg, 1911), p.
142.
    [2]For a detailed, eyewitness account of the activi-
ties of *The Northern Herald*, see L. Gurevič, "Istorija
'Severnogo vestnika,'" in *Russkaja literatura XX veka*,
Vol. I. Ed. S. A. Vengerov (Moscow, 1914), pp. 235-264.
    [3]The poet's wife, the critic and writer Anastasja
Čebotarevskaja, notes in her biographical sketch of her
husband ("F. Sologub: Biografičeskaja spravka," in
Russkaja literatura XX veka 1890-1910, Ed. S. A. Vengerov, Moscow, 1915, Vol. II, pp. 9-13), that his liter-

ary activity began considerably earlier than this time.
"(Sologub) wrote his first verse at age twelve
in 1875.   In 1879 he began to write a novel,
which was left unfinished.... At that time he
also began writing a theoretical tract about
the form of the novel.... He worked assiduous-
ly during this time, writing verse, translating the German poets Goethe and Heine, but
showed this to no one and sent it nowhere"
(p. 10).
[4]A. Belyj, "Privetstvie Fedoru Sologubu v den' jubi-
leja, 26 janvarja 1924," in CGALI (Moscow), fond 53, A.
Belyj, tom 1, ed. xr. 133, list 3. For a full account of
Belyj's relationship to Sologub, see S. Rabinowitz, "Bely
and Sologub: Toward the History of a Friendship," in
Gerald Janacek, ed., *Andrey Bely: Life and Work* (Lexington: University of Kentucky Press, 1978), pp. 156-168.
[5]E. Zamjatin, *Lica* (New York: Chekhov Publishing
House, 1955), p. 37.
[6]A. Belyj, Letter to F. Sologub, April 30, 1908, in
Ežegodnik rukopisnogo otdela Puškinskogo doma (1972), pp.
132-133.
[7]P. Ryss, Portrèty (Paris, 1924), n.p.
[8]A. Dolinin, "Otrešennyj: K psixologii tvorčestva
Fedora Sologuba," *Zavety*, No. 7 (1913), p. 85.
[9]V. Xodasevič, "Sologub," *Sovremennye zapiski,*
XXXIV (1928), p. 347.
[10]Gleb Struve, "Tri sud'by: III. Rycar' novogo
obraza," *Novyj žurnal*, XVII (1947), p. 204.
[11]Quoted by A. Izmajlov, *Literaturnyj olimp* (Moscow
1911), pp. 299-300.
[12]R. Ivanov-Razumnik, *"Pisatel'skie sud'by"* (New
York, Literaturnyj fond, 1951), p. 17.
[13]V. Ivanov, *Freedom and the Tragic Life* (New York:
Noonday, 1970), p. 95.
[14]Ljubov' Gurevič sheds some revealing light on the
seriousness with which Sologub regarded Dostoevskij in
the following reminiscence:
    "Several times I wanted to speak to (Sologub)
    eye-to-eye, and once, I was talking to him
    about Dostoevskij, and at that time his soul
    opened up in all its weightiness, and one felt
    in its secret depths a real sanctity."
Quoted in I. Jampol'skij, "F. Sologub: Pis'ma k L. Ja.
Gureviči A. L. Volynskomu," *Ežegodnik rukopisnogo otdela
Puškinskogo Doma,* 1972, p. 113.

[15] J. Malmstad, *Mixail Kuzmin: A Chronicle of His Life and Times. M. A. Kuzmin: Sobranie Stixov, III* (Munich: Wilhelm Fink Verlag, 1977), p. 207.
[16] G. Struve, op. cit., p. 205.
[17] For a brief but insightful analysis of the theme of destruction in Russian literature of the 1870s and 1880s, see G. Bjalyj, "Sovremenniki," in *Čexov i ego vremja* (Moscow, 1977), pp. 5-19.
[18] A. G. Gornfel'd, "Fedor Sologub," op. cit., p. 16.
[19] R. Poggioli, *The Poets of Russia* (Cambridge, Mass., 1970), p. 80.
[20] See particularly Ivanov-Razumnik's discussion, which culminates in the following remark: "...Sologub's attempt to believe in 'Holy Jerusalem,' to see the goal and meaning of life in the future or even in the trans- cendental world—ended in failure and a return to his former cold despair." R. Ivanov-Razumnik, "Fedor Solo- gub," in *O smysle žizni* (St. Petersburg, 1908), p. 34.
[21] Sologub himself, an intensely private person, strongly protested the use of biographical material in any discussion of his work. Responding to Modest Gof- man's request for some information about his life which was to be included in the latter's anthology of symbolist poetry, Sologub wrote: "No one needs my biography. A writer's biography should come only after critics and the public pay sound attention to his works—so far this has not occurred." Modest Gofman, *Kniga o russkix poètax poslednego desjatiletija* (St. Petersburg, 1908), p. 239.
[22] A. Gornfel'd, op. cit., p. 17.
[23] V. G. Kranixfel'd, *V mire idej i obrazov* (St. Petersburg, 1912), p. 9.
[24] M. Dikman, *Fedor Sologub - Stixotvorenija* (Lenin- grad, 1975), p. 22.
[25] A. Belyj, "Dalaj-lama iz Sapožka," *Vesy*, 3 (1908), pp. 63-76, and V. Xodasevič, op. cit. Note especially the latter's remark that "Spiritual progress is not to be found in Sologub's works" (p. 354).
[26] Čukovskij (K. Čukovskij, "Putevoditel' po Solo- gubu," in *Sobranie sočinenij v 6 tomax*, Moscow, 1969, VI, pp. 332-367), is yet another critic who argues against any evolution in Sologub's work.

CHAPTER I

THE STORIES:
CHILD AS HERO

Sologub's fame in the West rests primarily on his
reputation as a superb novelist, the author of *The Petty
Demon*, which continues the Gogol line of stylistically
complex and opaque prose, and, somewhat less so, as a
great poet who follows in the Pushkin tradition of classical simplicity. Yet his short stories, which are considerably less well-known, often reveal an equal measure
of greatness, and their best representatives show Sologub to be a master of—and in some cases an innovator
in—this genre. The difference between the stories and
the writer's works in other literary modes is largely a
formal one, for all of Sologub's writings share a few
basic themes and most reveal similar emotional responses
to a small group of recurring philosophical concerns.
The extension of these concerns to virtually all of his
major characters, regardless of genre—or age, has often
led readers to accuse Sologub of an obsessive preoccupation with his own subjective inner domain to the exclu-
sion of the outside realm of objective reality which he
shuns and fears.

Sologub's Manichaean vision of a splintered, imperfect world dominated by a constant play of opposites and
his attendant desire to escape to a private dream of
harmonious, incorruptible beauty pervades his entire literary corpus. Particularly striking is the fact that
from the beginning of Sologub's career profound metaphysical questions about the nature of life are combined
with an intense curiosity about the special world of
children. These characters predominate in the vast majority of Sologub's earliest short prose works written
between 1894 and 1898. To the fledgling writer, the
short story and the child were inextricably linked. It
is here that the child initially reveals his connection
to Sologub's central literary and philosophical concerns.

Some remarks about one of the best examples of
Sologub's short prose, the story "Dream on the Stones"
("Mečta na kamnjax," 1912), will clarify the child's relationship to Sologub's dualistic vision. The very title
suggests the opposing forces at work in this polarity:
"mečta"—dream, fantasy, legend, the world of the 'there'

is oddly predicated on 'kamen'"—stone, earth, reality,
the world of the "here." These are the two planes—the
ideal and the actual—between which Sologub continually
vacillates. His preoccupation with the former signifies
an allegiance to symbolist concerns, the etherealness and
abstractness of which the succeeding generation of poets,
the acmeists, would categorically renounce. Thus when
the time came for the acmeist poet, Osip Mandelstam, to
publish his first collection of verse (1913), he chose
the title *Stone* ("Kamen'"), as if to reinforce the new emphasis on concreteness, earthiness, and clarity.

   Of all Sologub's literary characters, his children
are particularly aware of the heaven-earth cleavage. The
twelve year-old Grishka is obsessively concerned with the
dual nature of things, and in the opening of the story,
with its pensive, philosophical tone, he ponders questions asked by many of Sologub's adult-heroes, as well as
the lyrical "I" of his poetry.

> Year after year passes, centuries pass and
> still the mystery of the world and the even
> larger mystery of man's soul is not revealed
> to man. He asks, he experiences, but he
> does not find the answer. The wise, such
> as children, do not know. And not even
> everyone asks, "Who am I?" (XIV, 51)[1]

   Grishka's unique wisdom is reflected in his consist-
ent philosophical inquiry into the sources and meaning of
his existence; it is defined by his sense of a divided
world and a split, disunited self. Prevalent in the
Sologubian child is an intuition that one's earthly self
or earthly existence is the incorrect and improper one.
Yet the corrolary to this belief—that there is a right
self or mode of being—exists equally strongly in these
characters' consciousness. Each one of them would sub-
scribe to Natasha Rostova's formulation in *War and Peace*,
that "when you remember, remember everything, you remember so far back that you remember what it was like before you were on this earth...."[2]
   The earth in "Dream on the Stones" is depicted in
terms of a crowded, noisy metropolis where the boy lives,
a constraining courtyard and a dank, dirty house—all of
which threatens the purity and spontaneity which the
child in Sologub usually embodies. Parental rebuke and
punishment of Grishka (he has broken a cup and is for-

bidden to play outside), which results in the restriction
of his physical movement, represents one of many examples
of what Sologub considers to be the earth-grounded
child's victimization. Grishka's extreme sensitivity to
life's fixity recalls a prominent motif in Sologub's
works—earthly imprisonment, which is sounded most grue-
somely in the poem which begins:

My - plennye zveri	We are captive beasts
Golosim kak umeem,	Crying as only we know how
Gluxo zaperty dveri,	to,
My otkryt' ix ne smeem.	The doors are shut tight
(1908)	And we are able to open
	them.

Children are the most poignantly depicted of Sologub's earthly prisoners; yet they do dare to escape from
their cages. Grishka attempts this via a persistent vision about a distant, happy land where everything is different from "these people whom he saw here in this boring
house which was like a prison, and in these tormenting
streets and side-streets and in this entire dull, northern capital" (XIV, 56). Continuing his fantasies on the
stone slab of the windowsill on a lower floor of the
building (hence the name of the story), because he is in
his mother's way, Grishka sees a beautiful palace and
recognizes the charming Princess Turandina who explains
that she has cast a spell over him, banishing him from
his princely home and making him the son of a cook.
Grishka begs to know who he is, but Turandina only
laughs and says that unless he himself can guess, he
will always be Grishka. Painfully aware of the incongruity between his beautiful distant land and the stuffy
kitchen in the dull city where he lives, Grishka can
only think of the question, "Who am I and why have I
forgotten my name? ... It is impossible that it is all
that. I can't really be only Grishka," (XIV, 62) he repeats.
     Yet, he will never be able to answer the question,
"Who am I?" and the profound metaphysical implications,
as well as the bitter tone of the story's last lines reveal a narrator who is as puzzled and tormented as his
child-hero:

Who am I, sent into this world by an unknown
will for an unknown purpose? If I am a slave,

then whence my power to judge and condemn,
whence my haughty schemes? If I am more than
a slave, then why does the ugly and false
world around me lie in evil? Who am I? The
cruel and no-longer beautiful Turandina laughs
at poor Grishka and at his dreams and futile
questions (XIV, 66).

The strongly-felt dichotomy between banal, everyday
reality and a more beautiful and attractive existence is
more obvious here than in any Sologubian story. Since
our present life is necessarily evil, the few earthly
reflections of beauty which contradict this state must
originate elsewhere. "Dream on the Stones" contrasts
quite sharply the child's vision of this ideal existence, from which he believes he has originated, with the
ugliness of the here-and-now.

It is precisely this world of the here-and-now, with
its constant abuse of the vulnerable youngster, which
constitutes the major focus of a group of stories that
might be subtitled "the child and life."* In the story
"Shadows" ("Teni," 1894), Sologub's first published prose
piece, which later appeared under the modified titles
"Light and Shadows" ("Svet i teni") and "The Wall and the
Shadows" ("Stena i teni"), a twelve year-old gymnasium
student gradually withdraws from his tedious home and
school life (the world of the "light") into the enchanting world of shades to which he is mysteriously and uncontrollably attracted. The shadows hint at an unknown
and hitherto undiscovered existence which Volodya—
and eventually his mother—come to understand. By the
final chapter of this haunting story, an initially harmless and naively curious fascination with a little game
of reflecting silhouettes on the wall culminates in an
obsessive preoccupation, a mad and hypnotic ecstasy which
renders mother and child totally passive and blissfully
oblivious to their external surroundings.[3]

In the story "Hide and Seek" ("Prjatki," 1898) it is
again a game which enables the child to escape this life
and retreat into another, more desirable existence. The

*Other stories which belong to this thematic cate-
gory include "The Smile" ("Ulybka," 1897);"Lel'kd" (1897);
"The Little Sheep" ("Barančik," 1898); "In Captivity"
("V plenu," 1905).

infant Lelechka constantly engages in hide-and-seek in
which either a certain part of the body "vanishes" merely
by covering it with one's hands or the entire person disappears by hiding. Not seeing any harm in the game which
arouses others' suspicions, Lelechka's mother contends
that "there can be no correspondence between a child's
amusement, which any child can enjoy, and the length of
its life" (III, 140). Yet by the end of the story Sologub proves the opposite: merry, cheerful, and beautiful
children are not destined for long life on this earth—
and Lelechka soon contracts a high fever and dies. Like
all of Sologub's special earthly children, Lelechka symbolizes a beauty and vitality which is foreign to this
life and which is fated to be short-lived. She is always
laughing and moving, and movement for Sologub—be it
dancing, jumping, or swimming—is the unquestionable sign
of that natural, spontaneous life-force which is prevalent particularly in children and which this earthly
existence stifles or destroys. Lelechka's desire to hide
or disappear is symptomatic of a commonly shared intuition of another world to which Sologub's children feel
they belong and to which they desire to return. Her
mother indicates an understanding of the game's real
meaning when she asks: "Why did Lelechka think about
(hiding) all the time? Didn't it all bore her? ... Perhaps Lelechka lacked a strong attachment to the earth
..." (III, 141-142).

The evil of earthly attachment is often epitomized
by the school, which at least in two stories "The
Cavalry Guardsman" ("Konnyj stražnik," 1907), and "The
Search" ("Obysk," 1908), causes the innocent child un-
told suffering. By leveling them to ordinary human dimensions, the school always bores Sologub's children; it
constantly stifles their imaginations, hampers their
freedom, and attempts to ensnare them in purely earthly
matters which alienate and threaten them. In the former
story, the deranged schoolteacher, Pereyashin, who
closely resembles Peredonov in *The Petty Demon*, arouses
one of his pupils from bed one night and leads him to
his study to be whipped. As is usually the case in
Sologub's stories, the distinction between the forces of
good and evil are sharply delineated. This is particularly evident when the teacher first eyes the sleeping boy,
"whose face had an innocent and significant expression,
as if he were dreaming about heavenly angels, who were
playing with golden balls on emerald green fields. And

the innocent, meaningful expression on his face irritated
Pereyashin" (XI, 143). In "The Search" a perfectly innocent schoolchild is forced to undergo a humiliating
search to prove that he has not stolen another pupil's
pen-knife. What is lightly dismissed by the wicked
schoolmaster and even the boy's mother becomes for Sologub an event of great psychological import, and the story
ends with a penetrating comment. "The degrading feeling
of the search remained with the boy. This feeling
pierced into him very much; after all, he was suspected
of thievery, searched and, feeling half naked, he was
swivelled around in the hands of an ambitious man" (XI,
173-174). Like Dostoevsky, Sologub realizes the seriously scarring effects such traumatic incidents have on an
individual's life. And his implication at the end of
"The Search" is clearly reminiscent of Dostoevsky's pre-
diction in *The Diary of a Writer*, when he claims: "Yes,
these children's souls did see somber pictures and they
are used to strong impressions, which, of course, will
forever be retained by them and which will come back to
haunt them all through their lives in dreadful dreams."[4]

     In its depiction of the extent and degree which hu-
man cruelty can reach, "The Youth Linus" ("Otrok Lin,"
1907) is unparalleled among Sologub's stories. Although
its ancient Roman setting may very well be a disguise
for what D. S. Mirsky believes is a contemporary "Revo-
lutionary story,"[5] its historicity imputes a more universal and general significance to the problem at hand.
There are neither temporal or geographical limits to
evil, nor are there restrictions on the people by whom
or on whom it is perpetrated. After mercilessly
slaughtering a rebellious segment of the population,
some Roman soldiers are at first reluctant to assign a
similar fate to a group of youngsters whom they observe
playing by the road. But the actions of one of these
children, "the beautiful boy Linus," alters this decision. Stepping away from the frightened children, Linus
shouts defiantly at the threatening troops: "Murderers!
Executioners! Tormentors of the innocent!" (XI, 115).
Against the advice of the other children, and with a
gesture which is characteristic of many of Dostoevsky's
child characters (e.g., the sexually abused Matryosha
shaking her fist at Stavrogin in *The Possessed*), Linus
lifts his hand, "small, powerless, clenched in a fist"
(XI, 115), and screams even louder: "Executioners! Executioners! How will you wash from your hands the blood

of those you have killed?" (XI, 115). Linus then moves
further apart from his playmates, to whom he confesses:
"I don't want to live in this detestable world, where
such cruel deeds are accomplished" (XI, 116). His request that only he be punished for his defiance is de-
nied, and as the sun "rejoiced from on high in this evil
earthly business, already preparing with the merciless
rays of its snake eyes to lap up the children's innocent
blood" (XI, 117), the soldiers butcher the entire group.

On one level "The Youth Linus" may be interpreted
as a parable about the ultimate triumph of good over
evil, where Linus's constant and miraculous reappearance
after death, to the increasing horror of the Roman soldiers, weighs heavily on their consciences and drives
them to suicide. But the story's major concern lies, as
usual, with the problem of the fate of beauty on this
earth. A helplessly small and powerless child, who is
always referred to as "prekrasnyj," represents beauty
and stresses its frailty and vulnerability on earth, as
well as its inability and unwillingness to survive in
this ugly, hostile world. This, of course, is the theme
of practically all of Sologub's stories where children
appear. Linus's defiance of the Roman soldiers, his
pronouncement that he does not "want to live on an earth
which the horses of your violent soldiers trample" (XI,
117), is perhaps the writer's clearest statement of the
irreconcilability of beauty and evil in this life—a
verbalization of sentiments shared by all of Sologub's
child-heroes.

Sologub's early stories immediately alert us to the
fact that at the core of his writing, as in Dostoevsky's,
there is often an acute struggle between thoroughly an-
tagonistic psychological forces (passive victims vs.
active victimizers) and seemingly incompatible philosophical antipodes (innocent beauty vs. harmful evil).
The resolution of these opposites would be a harmonious
coexistence for which Sologub strives throughout his entire career.

Significant as these clashes may be, they are rather
short on the kind of emotional intensity which Dostoevsky
so effectively conveys in his similarly inspired con-
frontations. Such high-pitched, feverish excitement
rarely exists in Sologub, but even when it does it is
undermined by a prose style that is largely characterized by Pushkinian lucidity and a classical sense of
measure and control. Violence, horror, and abuse exist

in "The Youth Linus," as images such as the soldiers'
horses sniffing the slaughtered children's smoky blood
while they slowly trample their dead bodies, remind us.
But beside, and almost to counter this, we have a style
which calls attention to the sheer beauty of its language
and which, because of its measured, deliberately poetical
diction, precludes the impassioned tonal quality frequently encountered in Dostoevsky's writing.

Take, for example, the extended description of the
centurion, who dreams of returning home from his brutal
pillaging and finding there his lovely captive slave
girls.

> Tol'ko izredka vstrečalis' bednye selenija s
> žalkimi lačugami—no, tomimyj tjažkim znoem,
> zabyl staršij centurion svoe namerenie obša-
> rit' vsju dorogu, i merno kačajas' na sedle,
> ugrjumo dumal o tom, čto končitsja kogda-nibud'
> ètot znoj, i dolgij put' pridet k koncu, i uve-
> dut boevogo konja, i voz'mut šlem i ščit, i pod
> širokim polotnom poxodnoj palatki budet proxlada
> i tixij svet nočnoj lampady, i opjat' zaplačet
> nagaja rabynja, i zaplačet svirel'nym golosom,
> žalujas' i pričitaja na čuzom i smešnom jazyke,
> i zaplačet, no budet celovat'. I on ee
> zalaskaet, zalaskaet do smerti—čtoby ne
> plakala, ne pričitala, ne žalovalas', ne govorila
> svirel'nym golosom ob ubityx, o milyx ej, o
> poveržennyx vragax velikogo Cesarja.

Only rarely did they encounter poor villages
with pitiful hovels, but the senior centurion,
exhausted by the oppressive heat, forgot about
his intention of pillaging along the way; and
rocking in his saddle rhythmically, he thought
sullenly of how that sultriness would have to
end sometime, and the long journey as well; and
then they would lead his warhorse off and take
his helmet and shield; and beneath the broad
canvas of his field tent there would be coolness
and the soft light of the night lamps, and again
the naked slave girl would begin to weep and she
would weep in a reedy voice, complaining and la-
menting in a foreign and humorous tongue, and
she would weep, but she would kiss him. And he
would caress her to death in order that she not

weep and not lament and not complain and not
speak in her reedy voice of the slain, of her
beloved ones, of the great Ceasar's fallen foes
(XI, 113).

This is a specimen of Sologub's poetic prose at its
best. The writing consists of long and syntactically
complex sentences, with their characteristic chains of
nominal and verbal modifiers, as well as rhythmic repetitions of similar words or grammatical units. In the
section which begins "i dolgij put'" ("and the long
journey"), we have a series of eight verbs in seven lines
("pridet," "uvedut," "voz'mut," "budet," "zaplačet,"
"zaplačet," "zaplačet," "budet celovat'"), all of which
but the last are preceded by the conjunction "i" ("and").
"Zaplačet" occurs three times, and other forms of alliteration or repetition are widespread: "put' pridet k
koncu" (the repetition of the consonant "p"); "i voz'mut
šlem i ščit" (the use of two sibilants, "š" and "šč"
consecutively); "i pod širokim polotnom poxodnoj palatki
budet proxlada" (a string of five words beginning with
the consonant "p" and frequently employing the vowel "a"
and "o", often in combination with the consonant "1").
The second sentence of the passage contains similar phenomena: "zalaskaet" used twice in a row; a series of
four verbs, each preceded by the negative particle "ne"—
"ne plakala, ne pričitala, ne žalovalas', ne govorila";
a string of three adjectives in the prepositional case,
modifying "vragax" ("enemies")—ob ubityx, o milyx, o
poveržennyx...."
This passage of sixteen lines contains only two sentences. The overall effect here, as in much of Sologub's
prose, is a sense of unhurriedness and weightiness. Furthermore, despite the initial complexity of these sentences, careful analysis demonstrates that they can be
broken down into smaller, terser units based on related
semantic clusters. Thus the intricacy and turbulence of
the whole is countered by the simplicity and controlled
tightness of its parts. So it is in the area of content.
The language is so calculated to achieve a lyrical and
musical effect that we tend to lose sight both of the
cruelness of the centurion, who two pages later will order the children's mass slaughter, and the pathetic situation of his slaves. The beautiful poetry not only
stands in stark contrast to the unpleasantness of the
situation, it serves to divert us from its full impact.

Any sense of heatedness comes from the sultry atmosphere,
which Sologub reinforces by the slow, languid pacing of
the prose, rather than from the angry, resentful, or
frantic tone of the language.

Dikman's observation of an earlier piece by the
writer, which she claims "maintain(s) a kind of 'simplicity' of style but ... combines it with a collision,
reminiscent of Dostoevskij,"[6] pinpoints the unique quality of Sologub's literary technique. Sologub's short
prose often constitutes a peculiar blend of metaphysical
ire and stylistic calm and poetic control. "The Youth
Linus" exemplifies such a phenomenon, perhaps explaining
why Mirsky singles out the story as "one of the most
beautiful pieces of modern Russian prose."[7]

To a significant degree, the above-mentioned stories
read like elaborations of Ivan Karamazov's litany of
child abuse before his rebellious reading of the *Legend
of the Grand Inquisitor*. Imprisoned by their earthly
existence, children are tormented by a wide range of
forces which Sologub is careful to define as inevitable
and unvanquishable. In this sense they are, like Ivan's
children, a movingly effective device for uncovering
life's irrational and terrible evil. Arguing Sologub's
inheritance of an important component of Dostoevsky's
philosophy by noting the similar use of the child to express and justify his metaphysical rebellion against the
insensitive laws of a dumb universe, Ivanov-Razumnik
claims:

> (Sologub) intentionally limits the field of his
> artistic creation by this circle (of children's
> suffering) just as Ivan Karamazov with the same
> circle outlined his ethical questions. And the
> reason is the same. The absurdity, meaningless-
> ness of life, its evil, its horror can be seen
> more clearly in children who still, speaking in
> Ivan Karamazov's words, have not eaten the apple
> and are still not guilty of anything.[8]

Yet beyond their purely ethical function and their
association with the cruel, drab here-and-now, children
indicate Sologub's countering vision of an ideal realm
of ethereal beauty. It is the child who, in Sologub's
shorter prose, consistently expresses the writer's
growing rejection of the empirical level of existence.
But this same character also conveys with equal persist-

tence Sologub's affirmation of another world, a world of
Platonic archetypes, which our physical reality only reflects. This pervasive and deeply divided world-view,
which sees life largely in terms of an unending struggle
between the forces of evil and their opposition, once
again recalls Dostoevsky. For Sologub's contrasting
philosophical outlooks range, if one speaks in terms of
Dostoevsky's culminating work, from Ivan's pessimism and
skepticism to Alesha's optimism and idealism. What makes
the connection between the two writers particularly
strong are the clear aesthetic parallels which exist between the Dostoevsky of *The Brothers Karamazov* and Sologub. In their common selection of children as a way of
demonstrating both their negative and positive vision of
the world, in their mutual dependence upon these characters to express their essential, though antithetical
metaphysical positions, the two are convincingly alike.

Ivan's rejection of God's universe comes on the
heels of a discussion concerning crimes against children
which, although "it reduces the scope of (Ivan's) argument to a tenth of what it would be,"[9] still forcefully
reveals the injustices and absurdities in which the
world abounds. Children especially appeal to Ivan because their angelic qualities increase the impact of his
argument. His selection of stories concerning their
suffering is understandable, for it is these sinless and
tormented souls who are the bane of his existence. "Do
you understand," he asks Alesha, "why this infamy must
be permitted? Without it, I am told, man could not have
existed on earth, for he would not have known good and
evil. Why should he know that diabolical good and evil
when it costs him so much? Why the whole world is not
worth that child's prayer to 'dear, kind God'! I say
nothing of the sufferings of grown-up people ... but
these little ones!"[10] Blameless children who are sub-
jected to barbaric cruelty prove the existence in the
world of unjustifiable evil, the presence of which defies all rational explanation and, consequently, destroys
the harmonious order by which Ivan wants the world to be
governed. The need for justice, whose absence he admits
would destroy him, prevents Ivan from accepting a world
where children's suffering remains unexplained. Ivan's
sense of justice outweighs his thirst for harmony, and
as long as unavenged evil exists, neither harmony nor
order is possible. The torture and suffering of innocent
children indicate to Ivan not only mankind's unmotivated,

irrational evil, but also, and perhaps more tragically,
God's utter lack of concern for the human condition. It
is this situation which convinces Ivan that happiness is
impossible in God's unjust world. As Mochulsky asserts,
"Ivan is proud of his reason and for him it is easier to
renounce God's world than reason."[11] This is precisely
what Ivan does. In reason's name he rejects the traditional God-centered universe with its necessary evil and
suffering and substitutes in its place the more humane
and comforting world of the self.

The phenomenom of man–God reflects an essential
philosophical parallel between Dostoevsky's fictional
character and Sologub, since it is responsible for the
strongly solipsistic tendency, particularly in the latter's poetry. It is here, as Dikman notes, that "re-
volting against God and rejecting Him, Sologub ... places
(human) personality in the center of the world's process,
(that) man—that 'I'—becomes God."[12] Ultimately Sologub and Dostoevsky lay great stress on depicting the
particular qualities of a godless world devoid of divine
light and moral sanity. Each ponders the metaphysical
ramifications of a world whose hopelessness is underlined
by the intolerable position of children. Both Sologub
and Ivan search for a rational, harmonious world based on
goodness and justice, where life is not arbitrary and
evil, but rather a meaningful and orderly system, which
is governed by truth and beauty. Each is quick to "hand
back the ticket," to reject this life, on the grounds
that the evil which forms an integral part of it is unacceptable.

Yet just as it is obvious that Ivan's is not the
only philosophical outlook which exists in *The Brothers
Karamazov*, so it is clear that Sologub's "Ivan Karamazov
side" represents merely one component of his *Weltanschauung*. Accordingly, in Sologub, as in Dostoevsky, children are not used solely as an excuse for rejecting life;
they serve as the very foundation upon which an alternative vision of the world is constructed. Alesha, who refuses to renounce the world on the basis of its existing
evils, preferring instead to view them in a positive
fashion, also represents a cogent world view, equally
valid as a response to life. In his case, Dostoevsky
uses children largely to convey this "upbeat" perspective. Invariably they are associated with such ideals
as faith, human compassion, and a striving for moral
beauty, and they permit Alesha to heed, in the true

spirit in which it is given, Zosima's admonition to "love
little children, for they are sinless, like little angels, and they are here to arouse tenderness, to purify
our hearts and in a sense to guide us."[13]   Alesha's attitude toward the dying schoolboy Ilusha demonstrates
best the significant ideological differences which exist
between himself and Ivan. Ilusha qualifies as a suffering victim of the world's evil every bit as much as
Ivan's tormented children. The boy's condition represents one of those ugly facts of life which are always
ready to haunt Ivan (as they do Sologub) and to serve as
ammunition for rejecting God's universe. Alesha, however, refuses to linger on the grief which Ilusha's pitiful situation elicits. He accepts the irrational basis
of life and neither tries to explain nor hopes to understand why children must suffer. Rather, he lets his
sorrow coexist with a faith in life which the child's
death actually helps to strengthen. The death of a
child does not cause Alesha to retreat inward. He does
not allow the anguished sadness he feels to act as a
catalyst for rejecting life's "absurdities" (the term is
Ivan's and, like Sologub's similar phrase, "fatal contradictions," it is used again and again). Such a positive reaction is possible only because Alesha understands
children not intellectually, as does Ivan, but intuitively. Choosing to stress the beauty of the child rather
than the evil which somehow permits it to die, Alesha
makes Ilusha's death into a redemptive memory for the
boys who are gathered at the deceased's tombstone.
Ilusha's death is, in a sense, a call to life, and it allows Alesha to make the fateful leap of faith equally
central in Sologub's world as it is in Dostoevsky's.

Ivan's focusing on the destruction of beauty leads
to his loss of faith and evokes feelings of skepticism
and rebellion. Alesha, on the other hand, marvels at the
very existence of beauty—a phenomenon which serves both
to increase his love of life and to produce his characteristic optimism. The child is invoked here to argue
the fundamental idea that belief is neither a rational
nor intellectual exercise. The basis for this belief—
beauty itself—although it surely exists, can be known
only intuitively. Sologub's search for this intuitive
beauty begins at the very outset of his career and it
constitutes the theme of one of the earliest specimens
of his writing.

Gde ty delas', neskazannaja
Tajna žizni, krasota?
Gde tvoja blagouxannaja,
Čistym svetom osijannaja,
Radost' vzorov, nagota?

Xot' by v dymke snovidenija
Ty poroj javilas' mne!
Xot' by postup'ju videnija
V kratkij čas uedinenija
Proskol'znula v tišine!

Where have you disappeared - you
Inexpressible secret of life - beauty?
Where is your sweet-smelling nakedness
Illuminated by pure light
And a joy to the eyes?

If only you would appear to me,
Even if in the haze of a dream!
If only, like the soft tread of a vision,
You would slip into the silence
During the brief hour of solitude.
(1885)

In Sologub, beauty—secret and frequently mysterious—is
very much a part of a divine world. In a group of
stories which deals largely with the child and nature,*
it is evident that both reveal hints of this Platonic
realm, the immutability of which is inevitably contrasted
to the temporality and changeability of the elements of
our ordinary material life.[14] Interestingly, the chronological span of these pieces shows Sologub's steady
movement away from the "here" to the comforting enchantments of the "there." Much of the action is restricted
to gardens, forests, parks, and the like—all of which
represent microcosms or earthly remnants of this divine
beauty; outside of these areas the Sologubian child cannot survive.

     *Several other stories by Sologub could be classi-
fied under this general heading: "To the Stars" ("K
zvezdam," 1896); "Earthly Back to Earth" ("Zemle zemnoe,"
1898); "The Tree Spirit" ("Elkič," 1906); "The White
Birch" ("Belaja berezka," 1909).

In "The Worm," ("Červjak," 1896), a young girl's
earthly sufferings gradually lead her to renounce life
and to return to the comfortable, sheltered fantasy world
of her early childhood. Because she has accidentally
broken a cup while merrily dancing around the boarding
house where she lives, the twelve year-old Wanda is
warned by the master that a worm will eat its way through
her entire body. The child is terrified. Gradually, and
with varying success, she attempts to divert her attention to her former idyllic life in the forest. At the
end of the story, plagued by the increasing discomfort of
the worm and becoming carried away by childhood memories
of her forest existence, Wanda dies, "a cruel smile dis-
torting her lips" (III, 74). The story describes the
child's ultimately successful attempt to ward off life's
evils and recapture the peace and comfort of the beautiful, idealized forest existence of her childhood. Wanda
has come to the Rubonosov household, i.e., to life,
harmless and pure. The breaking of the cup marks the
girl's official entry into the adult world; the master's
cruel threats and his symbolic transplanting of the worm
of evil into the child are, in a sense, part of the initiation ritual. Wanda's languishing signifies the
child's inability to assimilate evil, and her death,
which is symbolic of her refusal to enter adulthood, is
considered a victory. The greater life's threat the
stronger the child's resistance to it. What seems initially to be Wanda's losing battle is actually her strong
rejection of this world and the acceptance of its beautiful antithesis, the "secretly quiet, snow-covered forest" (III, 74). It is this dark, cool, and eternally
peaceful existence and not life's suffering and cruelty,
for which Wanda longs. In place of Volodya's amorphous
world of shadows ("Teni"), Sologub provides here the
initial strokes of his ideal realm of beauty, which he
expands in these first stanzas of a poem dedicated to
the poet Zinaida Gippius.

> Gde grustjat lesa dremlivye,
> Iznurennye morozami,
> Est' doliny molčalivye,
> Začarovannye grozami.
>
> Kak čuzda neposvjaščennomu,
> V sny mirskie pogružennomu,
> Ix krasa neobyčajnaja,

Neslučajnaja i tajnaja.

Where slumbering forests grieve,
Exhausted by winter frosts,
There are silent valleys,
Enchanted by storms.

How strange to the uninitiated,
Immersed in earthly dreams,
Is their unusual beauty,
So deliberate and mysterious.
(1895)

    Another of Sologub's nature stories, "The Snow
Maiden," ("Sneguročka," 1908), begins with an imaginary
dialogue between two children who cry when their recent-
ly-built snowmaiden melts. It continues with a detailed
reenactment of the events leading up to this situation in
the life of a brother and sister, Nyurka and Shurka, and
their parents, who represent the evil voice of skepticism
which denies the existence of the child's realm. Like
the majority of Sologub's children, Shurka and Nyurka are
alone in their special world, abandoned on this hostile
earth by some evil power which has left them here only to
suffer as they dream about this tempting but unreachable
life. An identical situation exists in "Dream on the
Stones." In fact, it is this same tormenting dilemma
which Sologub expresses in most of his works about children; if life is so ugly and evil, then why does beauty,
even though it is short-lived and doomed to destruction,
exist? Why is it here to entice and torture us? What
does it mean and where does it lead to? Sologub's writing is pervaded by a profound concern with the nature and
meaning of beauty; all of his works must ultimately be
evaluated on the basis of his current definition of, and
attitude toward, it.
    The creation of the snowmaiden takes place, predict-
ably, apart from everything else—in the children's miniature world of nature, "in which the amusing world of
the child's game, in the little garden, (which) was en-
closed from the street by a low fence" (XI, 223). They
are certain that the snowmaiden will play with them during this, and every winter, and "in spring (it) will
leave for the beautiful mountain where there is eternal
snow" (XI, 224). After much playing and frolicking, the

children and their friend (who has come alive when Shurka
kisses it) are called to tea. Although the father sees
before him a charming girl, all white and frozen, he does
not believe that she is made of snow and insists that she
come in and warm up by the fire. The act of leading the
snowmaiden into the house is symbolic, for it suggests
the adult's destruction of the child's created legend by
removing it from the world of beauty and imagination (the
garden), where it originated, into the grown-up world of
harsh, unimaginative reality (the house) where, of
course, it cannot survive. While both parents busily
fuss about looking for blankets, the snowmaiden slowly
melts until only a puddle of water remains on the floor.
Like the child, beauty flourishes best in its own secret
world from which it has come—that "high mountain" to
which the children want to go, quite away from and out of
contact with this life. The child has a special relationship with nature; both contain a common spirit which
feels imprisoned in this contaminated world which negates
the existence they previously knew. As the children's
new friend suggests, nature is not lifeless or inert; be-
low its serenely beautiful complexion lies a dynamic,
creative, and living essence, which for the sensitive and
knowing person has great meaning. For Nyurka and Shurka,
the snowmaiden is a genuinely living entity, the authenticity and excitement of which only they, as children,
can feel.

In "The Two Gotiks" ("Dva Gotika," 1906), the garden
and surrounding fields serve both as the scene of much of
the story's action as well as the locale which represents
and evokes for the child the beautiful world of his
dreams. Once again, nature is closest to the ideal world
of peace and beauty. Its comforting plushness and opu-
lence provide a refuge for the suffering individual; its
mystery and enchanting nocturnal loveliness contain a
completely new and undiscovered existence.

One summer night the young boy Gotik is aroused by
some noises, and when he looks out into the garden he is
amazed to see himself running about! There, under the
willow, is a schoolboy's figure, wearing Gotik's boots
and black trousers and dancing through the bushes and
trees in the direction of the river. Too tired to answer
his question, "But where am I going?", Gotik falls back
to sleep. The next morning he begins to recall "where
and why the second, nightly Gotik was going while he, the
first, ordinary and usual (Gotik) was lying in bed..."

(VII, 27). Gotik had dreamt of a quiet, magic castle,
completely illuminated by the moon's light, which exists
beyond an enchanted grove and in which the loving "moon
queen" Selenita lives. He has heard her speak and beckon
him with a voice that sounds like the current of a
stream, like the tender ring of a reed pipe, and he is
convinced that this is where the other Gotik has headed.
Excited by this marvelous sense of bifurcation, Gotik
thinks: "How good it is that there is another life, a
nightly, wonderful life which is like a fairy tale, another life besides this daily, crude, sunny, and boring
life. How good it is that it is possible to transfer
oneself to another body, to split one's soul, to have
one's own secret, hidden from everyone.... At night
everything is different. Day spirits sleep, they lie
with immovable bodies—and then come forth other, inner
spirits which during the day we don't know" (VII, 32).
However, Gotik's dream and the story itself end abruptly
when the maid comes forth and owns up to the deed: It was
she who dressed up as Gotik as part of a night-time masquerade with her friends. "The wonderful night life, and
Selenita, and everything which wasn't—really wasn't!
All that mystery was explained so simply and vulgarly"
(VII, 49), the child is forced to admit. Realizing that
he will never reach the beautiful land of Selenita,
Gotik breaks out into tears, and the narrator concludes
the work with an expression of his own frustration:

> Farewell my other unknown and secret life!
> I must live a boring and ordinary existence,
> and when night falls, I must sleep a sense-
> less, painful sleep (VII, 50).

"The Two Gotiks" is unique in its graphic representation of a concept which appears in most of Sologub's
stories. The piece suggests, and Gotik believes, that
there exist two sides within the individual: a diurnal,
earthly self (the "svet") and a sidereal, nonearthly
self (the "teni"). Sologub-the-poet, in whom this duality of selves is so painfully felt, reveals the importance of this cleavage to his entire psyche in a quatrain
which is in essence the departing point for all his work:

> Kakoj-to xitryj čarodej
> Raz'edinil moe soznanie
>   S prirodoju moej,—

I v ètom vse moe stradanie.

A certain cunning sorcerer
Separated my consciousness
    From nature, —
And herein lies the reason for my suffering.
(1896)

In Sologub's prose it is the child who most consistently expresses this sense of disjointedness due to a
rude detachment from a fuller, more vital existence whose
mysteries and joys he longs to know. No one more effectively conveys the anguish of being deprived of beauty,
of being irrevocably split off from a world of harmony
and unity than this character. Beautiful nature is part
of the same world as the nightly self with which man
steadily loses contact during the passage of time. Since
children are closer to this world, they perceive the
dichotomy between the earthly and nonearthly existence
more keenly than adults, whose sensitivity toward nature
and beauty is greatly dulled. Like the poet above, children feel that they are only partially awake in this
life, bewitched by an evil power which has removed them
from their native land and has concealed from them part
of their consciousness. Ironically, it is at night,
when the child should be sleeping, that he feels awake
and closest to his real self, hints of which he has
found in nature.

Sologub's pre-Revolutionary prose and poetry are
pervaded by a profound and often obsessively mournful
sense of loss—a uniquely *fin-de-siècle* theme, which is
treated with commensurate pathos in much of Annensky's
poetry and Bunin's prose. But the same works of Sologub
are also filled with a yearning for reconciliation, a
striving toward reunification with a world whose beauties
are felt increasingly to be an integral part of the
author's search for wholeness and self-definition. The
theme of man's tie to wondrous nature and his sense of a
special correspondence he has with the forces that animate it, a theme which is often associated with English
and German romanticism, becomes a modernistic concern as
well, especially in French literature, which Sologub
knew intimately. Along these lines, Gerard de Nerval's
statement in *La Rêve et la Vie* (a title significantly
reminiscent of Sologub's "Mečta na kamnjax"), is especially pertinent. Nerval's words capture a sentiment

shared by Sologub and relayed most frequently through his
children in stories whose very titles, "In Captivity,"
"To the Stars," "Earthly Back to Earth," seem to be an-
ticipated in the Frenchman's remark:

> "How is it," I said to myself, "that I can
> possibly have lived so long outside nature,
> without identifying myself with her! All
> things live, all things are in motion, all
> things correspond; the magnetic rays emanating
> from myself or others traverse without obstacle
> the infinite chain of created things; a trans-
> parent network covers the world, whose loose
> threads communicate more and more closely with
> the planets and the stars. Now a captive on
> this earth, I hold converse with the starry
> choir, which is fleetingly a part of my joys
> and sorrows."[15]

The sense of reconciliation expressed in Sologub's
nature stories is part of a larger pastoral vision which
contains decidedly Dostoevskian resonances. Remarkably
akin to Dostoevsky's concept of "living life" ("živaja
žizn'," a term which Login, the protagonist of *Bad
Dreams*, actually uses) and to his perception of paradise
described in "The Dream of a Ridiculous Man," this state
implies an anti-urban, Edenic life of moral and physical
purity, a kind of preconscious existence when everything
in the world was eternally fresh and new.

As Sologub's interest in childhood would suggest,
there is a great mistrust of time, history, and progress
in his works. The passage of time, which always signifies destructive change, invariably carries negative
associations. In this regard, Dikman notes that the
writer "prefers timeless myth, legend, and fairy tale to
history. He does not search for 'the bonds of time,'
but on the contrary, he aspires to forgetfulness ...
with (which) is connected the pessimistic assertion of
changelessness, the repetition of everything—all of
which signifies for Sologub the very tragically felt
theme of the 'eternal return.'"[16] Demonstrating the
writer's persistent concentration on a past era currently
lost and distant, but no less pure and desirable, the
child exemplifies Sologub's interest in the theme of
eternal return. This character's continual appearance in
his works suggests that the concept of *illo tempore* was

never able to be eradicated fully from Sologub's consciousness. A thorough investigation of this topic would
constitute a major undertaking and would necessarily involve comparison with Nietzsche, whose influence on Sologub was considerable.[17] Yet, it is still evident that
the idea of abolishing history and devaluating time, of
returning to the mythical moment of creation in order
to experience regeneration, of continually recreating
life by recapturing the past, is embodied most firmly in
Sologub's literary children. The importance in Sologub's
thinking of the notion of "eternal return" and its many
ramifications becomes obvious in a group of stories where
the lure of death is particularly strong among children.
Such attraction is important and highly complex in Sologub; suffice it to say at present that to the Sologubian
child death means a termination of life's corruptive
forces, a defeat of time and process (whence the title
of Sologub's drama, *The Victory of Death (Pobeda smerti*,
1908), and a subsequent return to his original source of
being, to his pre-conscious life.

"Consolation" ("Utešenie," 1897) is a story which
Sologub's wife, the critic and author, Anastasya Chebotarevskaya, singles out as "probably the most convincingly
and most characteristically developed (example) of the
author's pessimistic theory."[18] It tells of how a thirteen year-old's fascination with death steadily increases
until he himself decides to commit suicide. A little
girl's accidental death, which the hero, Mitya Darmostuk,
witnesses as he is walking home from school one day, is
the unforgettable incident which brings the boy face-to-
face with something he had never thought about and which
also serves as a catalyst for his gradual, but ultimately
total change in attitude toward life. Mitya cannot remain indifferent to Raechka's passing, and the notion of
death becomes more and more pleasant as it moves him further away from his former worldly concerns. Thinking
about Raechka in heaven, he decides that she is far better off there: "And if Raechka grew up, she would have
been a housemaid ... and is there any real beauty here
anyway?" (IV, 38, 39). The girl begins to remind Mitya
of death and she beckons him to her. "Wasn't she herself
death? Beautiful death! Then why life? (IV, 70). This
critical question indicates the child's realization that
in the face of the eternally "frozen" beauty which
Raechka represents, life is senseless. Why continue
this painful existence when he can follow the girl's

path of earthly negation? The story's title signals the
consoling force which opposes and arrests life's inevitable destructiveness and which transports the child from
this ugly world to a peacefully changeless state, the
harmoniousness of which the girl's name, "raj"—paradise
—suggests. As Raechka shows, death has a truth all its
own, and in "Consolation" it is this, rather than the
beauty of nature, toward which the child strives.

Viewed against the background of "Consolation," the
above-mentioned stories which do treat death, reveal a
wholly different approach toward the same phenomenon.
The primary focus in "Hide and Seek" is not on death's
ability to return Lelechka to that heavenly world from
which she has come (as is the case in "Consolation"),
but rather on its role as the epitome of life's hostility
toward her beauty. In "The Youth Linus" as well, the
child's death points to the extent of life's evil instead
of representing a possible alternative toward it. As we
observe, Sologub's attitude toward death can be contradictory, for it is seen both negatively—as the most
terrible force working against the child, the culmina-
tion of life's evil, and positively—as a welcome escape
from these very evils and as a gift of great value.
Thus, death is regarded not only as life's most appalling
consequence, but at times as its greatest blessing.

In no story are these views of death better juxta-
posed than in "The Sting of Death" ("Žalo smerti," 1903).
The biblically-inspired epigraph, "the sting of death is
sin" (I Corinthians 15-16), captures the essence of
Sologub's attitude toward death at this stage of his
career. To feel death's hurt, to associate it with pain,
is wrong; for, as his children come to know, death is a
blissful emancipation from the imprisonment of earth's
material bonds, a process in the reestablishment of his
once-possessed freedom. The boys for whom death becomes
a friend are two school children, Vanya and Kolya, whose
personalities are completely different. The former "had
something distorted, something repressed and evil ... appearing in his face" (IV, 109), while the latter immediately appears handsome. Kolya is further distinguished
by the fact that he lives alone with his mother; Sologub's positive child-heroes almost always lack one par-
ent, a condition which causes—and symbolizes—a greater
weakening of their earthly allegiance. Never firmly se-
cured in the family unit, the child is less earth-bound
and, consequently, more prone to other worldly attrac-

tions. The boys' story depicts the struggle, in almost
allegorical fashion, between the forces of evil (life)
and good (beauty), in which the latter's victory is
guaranteed solely by its escape from the former by means
of death. Vanya's leading of Kolya early in the story
to his favorite spot in the forest, a dark and narrow
trench, is a harbinger of the boy's impending fall from
innocence. Falling under Vanya's harmful influence,
Kolya forfeits his purity through a series of initiations
into the vices of adult life. The reaction of Kolya's
mother to her son's drunken arrival home one night leads
to Vanya's humiliating thrashing, which in turn results
in his malicious idea of revenge against his informer.
His decision to convince Kolya to drown himself is the
ultimate evil which Vanya (life) inflicts upon the boy.
In keeping with Sologub's penchant for personifying ab-
stractions, we might say that "The Sting of Death" is an
allegory about how, after leading the child further along
its abominable path, the evil forces of life finally decide to kill it.

Although Vanya's vengeful scheme may be viewed negatively, Kolya's demise has its positive aspects insofar
as death serves to liberate him from tormenting life.
Moreover, it is precisely the threat of death and suffering which spur the child on to seek a more comforting alternative in the first place. Thus, in Kolya's case,
death is at once an affliction and a joy. "Kolya lis-
tened and believed ... and death, comforting, peaceful,
soothing life's sadness and distress, became more desirable and beautiful .... Death is genuine and eternal,
eternally unchanging life. It offers another form of
life and it does not deceive" (IV, 143). Vanya's reasons
for dying are so convincing that he himself joins Kolya
in suicide, and in the last scene the boys' double drown-
ing is related. The sudden change to a more positive attitude toward death, which occurs at the end of "The
Sting of Death," reflects a more general trend in Sologub's work as a whole, which Georgette Donchin has
noted. "In his early days ... Sologub can only express
fear of the inevitability of death, and all his thoughts
are controlled by this fear mingled with despair. But
then Sologub discovers that life and not death is something to be afraid of, and after this volte-face, he becomes the most expressive chanter of death among all the
Russian Symbolists."[19] One of Sologub's strongest statements on the subject, "The Sting of Death" describes

death's significance as an escape from the bondage of
earthly suffering to a changeless state, free from the
laws of physical reality and necessity. So alluring is
this condition that even those who are satisfied by and
entrenched in this life cannot resist its power. The
fact that children convey the idea of passive resignation
from earthly longing and activity—so central a concept
in Sologub's metaphysical system—again attests to their
importance in the writer's prose. It is they who demonstrate most graphically in the fiction Sologub's connection to the German philosopher, Artur Schopenhauer (1788-
1860). The latter's teachings about withdrawal from the
world of evil, cessation of bodily desire, and purgation
of worldly yearning are very often realized in, if not
openly expounded by, the Sologubian child.[20] Particularly in the stories which concentrate on death, children
are presented as the greatest resisters against the impulse of passion and as the most vocal spokesmen against
volition in general.

In analyzing the child's relationship to nature and
death, we suggested a particular cosmogonic scheme which
forms the basis of Sologub's world view, yet the only
direct statement on the subject came at the outset of our
discussion when we stressed the dualistic nature of this
highly idiosyncratic vision. Although it is obvious that
for Sologub, children represent a special kind of beauty,
the reasons for the uniqueness of this quality and also
for the child's singular relationship to it can be fully
appreciated only upon reviewing "The Art of Our Day"
("Iskusstvo našix dnej," 1915).[21] This essay stands as
the writer's clearest and most comprehensive statement
regarding his conception of the world and the kind of art
necessary to describe it. By 1912-1913 the "crisis of
symbolism" was becoming obvious as the predictions of its
proponents about art's ability to transform reality were
losing credibility and as other literary schools began to
develop in reaction to the movement. To defend the goals
of symbolism and to ensure its continuing acceptability,
Sologub made a whirlwind tour of the provinces in 1912-
1913, lecturing on the material, which he eventually published as "The Art of Our Day."'

As Sologub sees it, reality, i.e., the natural environment and the living beings who inhabit it, exist and
function on two separate levels which, when properly perceived, can be completely interrelated. The first and
most readily observable plane of existence, the material

world, consists only of visible, tangible, and finite
phenomena which appear independently and in total isolation of one another in the immediately perceivable present. These "independent" entities are all slavishly
bound and narrowly limited by the very spatial and temporal constraints which define their deceptively autono-
mous existence. Sologub contends that no single phenomenon possesses its own integrity, existing in and of itself, apart from all other phenomena which surround it.
Thus the notion, popular among naturalist writers, that
life is the sum of all independent and unrelated phenomena whose existence depends on what is, in truth, an extremely limited ability to perceive them, is preposter-
ous. Reality cannot and should not be understood or explained exclusively on the basis of the sensations and
observations which are most readily available to man.
Such a completely erroneous perception of one's surroundings tarnishes man's ideals. Such a fallacious definition of one's existence provides man with only "a world
of phenomena where everything which appears to the naked
eye ... is doomed to decay, exhaustion and destruction
even before death comes, (where) all is doomed to depravity, all living things (are) forced to feel the lie
and evil of life."[22]

Sologub rejects what he believes is the disaster of
an exclusively materialistic world-view. Consequently,
he defines reality as the multi-leveled, multi-dimen-
sional interrelationship and coexistence of objects
which, transcending customary spatial and temporal
boundaries, extend far beyond the reaches of immediate,
"logical" perception. Phenomena, animate or not, do not
exist "independently" and autonomously. Beneath and beyond their visible surface lies an essence ("suščnost'")
which is part of, and thus a link to, a much larger omni-
present force which pervades, controls, and guides
everything. The possession of this one essence by all
phenomena ultimately destroys their individual integrity,
makes them mutually dependent and totally interconnected,
and produces a world which is cohesively and organically
unified. All phenomena, as common manifestations of the
all-powerful, all-unifying One, are fused together in a
harmonious world of matter and spirit where every action
has repercussions throughout the entire system. And
that divine force or essence which only occasionally reveals itself, and then only in hints, represents and
points to Sologub's world of absolute beauty. It is

this force which ultimately unites and gives meaning to
everything on earth. Each phenomenon, at least potentially, possesses it to a larger or smaller degree.

Sologub also strongly censures the temporal limitations which are associated with the traditional conception of reality. Just as on the spatial level the
existence of any object or person, although seemingly
the sum of his visible, tangible parts, in truth extends
far beyond its artificial limitations, so on the temporal
plane, currently existing phenomena, particularly human
beings, transcend their "present" boundaries. Instead,
these phenomena function as the simultaneous integration
and interrelationship of past, present, and future and at
all times have the power to reach back to the past or act
as the embodiment of the future. That beauty,which, on
the spatial level, is concealed beneath all immediately-
perceived phenomena, exists, on the temporal level, in a
distant, remote past—"in the beginning"—which is part
of, although usually camouflaged by, the immediate present. And since present, past, and future are all contained
within man, this original beauty lies well within his
grasp; he need only learn how to reach it.

A conception of reality where each object contains
and represents an entire series of other possibilities,
where the infinite at all times is contained in the
finite, requires an appropriate aesthetic. This Sologub
defines as a method in which "the artistic image provides
the greatest possibility of penetrating its meaning ...
(and) arouses in the soul of the perceiver the extensive
compiling of thoughts, feelings, and moods, more or less
indefinite and multi-meaningful.... It is then that the
depicted object becomes a symbol."[23] Understandably, the
only acceptable aesthetic for Sologub is one in which
"objects of this transient world are represented not in
their separate arbitrary existence, as in naturalism, but
in the general relationship not only between themselves,
but with a wider world than our own."[24]   Consequently,
the artist must show how each image of the objective
world is a "window opened to infinity." He needs to
demonstrate that phenomena are a part of the material
world in which they are initially perceived and that they
belong to and reveal an infinite, eternal world beyond
this existence. Poetically, Sologub would express this
belief in the lines: "In the limitlessness of space /
somewhere there is another world" ("V bespredel'nosti
prostranstva / gde-to est' zemlja inaja").

In comparing the symbol (and, by extension, symbolist art) to a window through which one is transported
from the banal reality of earthly existence to the transcendent world of infinity and absolute beauty, Sologub
may have been inspired by Mallarmé's famous poem "The
Windows" ("Les Fenêtres," 1863).[25] As the dividing point
between two perspectives on life—the external condition
of earthly sickness, mortality, and oppressive constraint
verses the internal impulse toward perfection, timelessness, and unrestricted freedom—the French poet's window
signifies the dual function which Sologub believed every
symbol should possess. Yet, despite their possible ties
to Mallarmé, Sologub's theoretical statements, as well as
their application in his art, show a far more important
connection to the teaching of Vladimir Solovyov, who argued (to quote James West) "that art should reveal the
relationship in which the phenomenal world stands up to
the ultimate reality."[26] Sologub defines in "The Art of
Our Day" and upholds in much of his fiction, particularly
where children are involved, one of the basic tenets of
symbolism largely characteristic of the younger and more
philosophically oriented members of the movement—Bely,
Blok, V. Ivanov—with whom Sologub is not customarily
associated. Such a tenet discounts the existence of a
single empirical level of reality and rejects exclusive
loyalty to the visible world. Rather it recognizes a
transcendental order which forms an integral part in the
totality of human experience. Representing more than
merely a literary technique or protest against traditional forms of literary expression, symbolism, as
Sologub describes it here, acknowledges, and systemati-
cally attempts to fathom the meaning of, the higher realm
which lies beyond the phenomenal. It argues for the
ultimate interconnectedness of all things, for the essential harmony among seemingly disparate elements, and
for their final allegiance to a higher unity (Sologub's
Schopenhauerian inspired "One Will")—all of which is
perceived intuitively. Sologub's belief in Solovyov's
"ultimate reality," his preoccupation with an "absolute
principle," form the basis of his symbolist art, which
will "inevitably lead to the meaning of life,"[27] i.e.,
to the eternal and harmonious beauty which the hidden
world ultimately represents. And to the extent that his
art reflects a desire to comprehend life by reaching the
essence of its hidden truths, Sologub can be justifiably
associated with the second generation of symbolists.

These are the writers who used the symbol, in Ivanov's
words, to "reveal in the objects of everyday reality ...
signs of another reality (and) enable us to become aware
of the interrelationship and the meaning of what exists,
not only in the sphere of earthly, empirical consciousness, but in other spheres, too."[28]

In the light of these definitions of symbol as well
as the description of Sologub's unique cosmogonic scheme,
there is no doubt that the figure in Sologub's works who
most directly embodies the essence which lies hidden beneath all earthly phenomena and which ultimately leads to
the world of infinite beauty is the child. It is he who
is Sologub's clearest and most unambiguous symbol. When,
in "Shadows," Sologub tells us that for his first literary child "objects themselves no longer interested (him),
he almost ceased to see them, all his attention was cen-
tered on their shadows" (I, 27), he is setting into mo-
tion a characteristic which is common to all his positive
children: their ability to penetrate beyond their everyday existence into the hidden, enchanting world of es-
sences. The child in Sologub is usually seen as part of
this nonearthly world. He stands as a microcosm which
represents the macrocosm, serving as living proof of the
existence of this divine, albeit secret life. The beauty
of this world, like Sologub's children themselves, does
not totally exist on this earth nor does it wholly belong
to it. And the fact that the child reveals only a part
of this essence is not surprising, for according to
Ivanov, "a symbol is a genuine symbol only when it ...
utters in its secret ... language hints and sugges-
tions."[29]   As Carlyle asserts, it is important only that
"in the symbol proper ... there is ever, more or less
distinctly and directly, some embodiment and revelation
of the Infinite; the Infinite is made to blend itself
with the Finite, to stand visible and, as it were, at-
tainable there."[30]

The children whom we have thus far discussed are
clearly seen to have originated in that other "infinite"
world; consequently, their unique beauty is neither native to, nor fully comfortable in, our present phenomenal existence. Strangers to this earth, Sologub's
children are initially unfamiliar with life's evil. Each
story focuses on the child's increasing awareness of his
naïvité as he is gradually separated from the world where
he originated, and as he becomes more integrated into a
corrupted, spiritless material life. Volodya's shadows

represent Sologub's earliest recognition of the divine,
ethereal world of beauty to which the child is consciously or subconsciously drawn. The critic Modest Gofman was
the first to explain this relationship.

> Sologub's main interest, the central point
> of his experiences and his obsession, is man's
> spiritual life. Behind our daily conscious-
> nesses, incessantly sweeping by it with its
> wave, lives and moves another; our pre-con-
> sciousness - senselessly wise, elemental,
> ancestral. By it we are associated with our
> furthest ancestors, through it our life and
> the soul of nature circulate spontaneously in
> us; like an underground spring it feeds all
> our psychic life. There are predisposed or-
> ganisms (*especially among children*) in which
> this preconsciousness uninterruptedly crosses
> with the everyday, normal consciousness.[31]

The sensitive person can detect within life's cruelty and
meaninglessness signs of another world of indestructable
beauty. In the following poem this beauty, represented
in the figure of the child, becomes an essential source
of hope and solace for the ailing, earth-bound poet.

> Net, ne odno tol'ko gore,-
> Est' na svete
> Alye rozy i zori,
> I bezzabotnye deti.
>
> Pust' v nebesax dogorajut
>   Zori tak skoro
> Pust' naši rozy ronjajut
>   Skoro ubory,
>
> Pust' omračajutsja rano
> Vlastiju zla i obmana
>   Detskie vzory,-
> Rozy, i zori, i deti
> Budut na pasmurnom svete.
>
> No, not only grief exists,
> There are also red roses and daybreaks
> And light-hearted children
> In the world.

Let each dawn fade away
Quickly in the heavens,
Let our roses quickly shed
Their petals.

Let the children's gazes
Be darkened early
By the power of evil and deceit.
Roses and dawns and children
Will always exist in our dreary world.
(1895)

Meeting all the requirements of Ivanov's above-
quoted definition of a symbol, the child—very much a
part of our everyday, material existence—also contains
that super-real and extra-terrestrial essence which,
under close scrutiny, points to a different reality. The
child himself is a "window opened to infinity" because
through him a more beautiful, more enduring, and eternally unchanging existence is often revealed.

For example, in "To the Stars," Sologub portrays a
child whose gaze is fixed increasingly upward to the enchanting, incorruptibly beautiful cosmic realm of the
stars. Serezha's gradual loss of his earthly groundings
is accompanied by an increased sense of attachment to the
special kind of otherness which he alone senses. So, in
"Earthly Back to Earth," where again the child's special
vision penetrates the fixed and limited dimensions of
material reality and looks beyond to a realm of expanded
consciousness. Like so many of their counterparts, these
children function as the medium through which Sologub
communicates his transcendent vision. By allowing the
free play of their imaginations, children, as it were,
provide air to the closed, stultifying world of routine
as they suggest an escape from an existence which is
ruled exclusively by the laws of necessity.

On one level, Sologub's children are believably
real, "normal" earthly human beings who participate in
everyday activities while, on another level, they per-
sonify the hidden, nonearthly existence of infinite
beauty. The combination of these two levels allows the
child to represent ideally Sologub's vision of a dual-
leveled reality. Indeed, the writer's use of the child
as symbol conforms exactly with Volynsky's definition of
the new art of symbolism, which, in his words, "is the
artistic combination of the world of phenomena with the

secret world of the divine."[32]

Sologub's insistence that the artistic image, before it becomes a symbol, "must itself be precisely depicted, so that it is not an arbitrarily and whimsically contrived image,"[33] and his contention that symbolism is the highest form of realism are borne out in his own symbolic depiction of the child. His children always function in the expected and quite natural milieux of nature, the home, or the school while they simultaneously live in their own special world. Sologub often describes the child's individual physical attributes with great care, and the world of phenomena to which this character belongs is depicted with unquestionable exactness of detail. This unabashed realism—with its precision and frequent attentiveness to the minutiae of life—distinguished Sologub from the majority of his modernist contemporaries. Despite a professed allegiance to the subjectivism, imaginativeness, and idealism of the generation of symbolists with whom he is rightly associated, he nevertheless insisted that the writer "approach humbly the phenomena of life ... (and) accept and affirm to the last everything in the phenomenal world...."[34] It was this firm grounding in the realist tradition which prompted Bryusov to observe that "we 'decadents,' we practitioners of the 'new art' are all somehow removed from everyday reality, from that which nowadays one loves to call real, truthful life ... (yet) among us F. Sologub is one of the few who has preserved a vital, organic tie to the earth.... He is at home as well here on earth."[35] Sologub himself hardly needed to be reminded of this quality of his writing. His early awareness of such an "earthiness," his concern over the necessary presence of the "real," even in his most idealistic creations, is reflected with abundant clarity in the subject matter and the very title of a collection of his earliest stories, *Earthly Children (Zemnye deti)*, whose prologue clarifies the child's status:

> Zemnye deti šalovlivy,
>   No kryl'ja est'
> O tom, kak angely ščastlivy,
>   Doxodit vest'.

> Earthly children are naughty,
>   But they have wings
> And so we know

That the angels are happy

What Sologub acknowledged in his children and what
he required of their portrayal, Ivanov, with his distinction between realistic and idealistic symbolism, fully
condoned. Ivanov was the last to disparage a loyalty to
a higher reality. But before the essence of things could
be understood, before one could be directed to what he
called, following Solovyov, "the religious idea," the
phenomenal world, whence all these strivings began, had
first to be faithfully and fully depicted. An art which
was not distinguished by realism and by a "faithfulness
to things as they are both in appearance and in essence,"[36] could never be truly symbolist for Ivanov.
This was rather decadent art (in Ivanov's terms, "idealistic symbolism") which, because it stressed illusion,
aestheticism, and loss of reality, could never ultimately
capture the symbolist goal of conveying "the reality of
the religious and mystical experience."[37]   The critic D.
Talnikov's fear that in proceeding to the realm of transcendental reality the symbolist might totally bypass the
empirical level, could not apply to Sologub's fiction.
Consequently, in his article "Symbolism or Realism," he
correctly emphasized that Sologub's symbolism was "almost
in the spirit of the old 'realistic art.'"[38]   Invariably
anchored in the phenomenal world, the child in Sologub
exemplifies an artistic method which reflects, as Dikman
argues, "(the writer's) inherent desire to preserve an
everyday ('bytovaja') and, for the most part, a psychological concreteness."[39]
        Yet insofar as symbolism's task was "to unite the
eternal, intransient with the temporal, with the world of
phenomena,"[40] the symbol had to contain within it those
above-mentioned "signs of another reality." It needed to
carry life's meaning beyond its immediate significance
and to direct the reader's attention away from the concrete and literal. Sologub certainly favored the creation of an exact sense of things through realism. On
this score, Dikman appropriately reports the writer's
assertion that "by bent of mind and by the peculiarities
of my education, I am much more an advocate of exact
knowledge, than I am a mystic."[41]   But the mystical belief in a transcendental reality was hardly foreign to
Sologub, and when discussing it, he conceded that "this
is for me not a matter of the mind, but a matter of conviction, and my entire life perception demands this

faith."[42]   Appropriately, his art also reflects the limitations of realism both in fathoming the ultimate meaning
of reality and also in evoking from the reader an emotional response, which he believed genuine art needed to
accomplish. He simultaneously admitted this shortcoming
and revealed its remedy when, in an article devoted to
defending modernist techniques in art, he wrote: "Decadence uses words and their combinations not as mirrors
for repeating the phenomenal world, but only as an in-
strument for arousing in the reader a certain internal
process."[43]   The words and images, which are combined to
produce Sologub's description of children, perform this
function admirably.

Both in his untainted, other-worldly purity and in
his special relationship with nature—not with ordinary,
inert nature, but with a world bristling with movement
and activity—the child reveals this hidden, intuitive,
though equally valid existence. In so doing, to quote
Volynsky, "the visible and the invisible, the finite and
the infinite, the sensibly real and the mystical are
fused together in an indissoluble unity, as the inalien-
able signs of two interconnected worlds."[44]   Sologub's
children belong to two worlds, and with one and the same
image the writer uncovers both the evils of the earthly
and material and the beauties of the divine and spiritual. Here he carefully follows Coleridge's definition
that "a symbol ... is characterized ... above all by the
transluscence of the eternal through and in the temporal.
It always partakes of the reality which it renders intel-
ligible, and while it enunciates the whole, it abides itself as a living part of that unity of which it is the
representation."[45]   Although the image of the child is
unambiguously precise and deliberate, quite reflective of
the realism of which Sologub said it had to partake, what
the child points to is, as Sologub thought it should be,
infinite, suggestive, and complex. Unlike the precisely
depicted phenomenal level, the second plane, the hidden
world from which the child has come and to which he ultimately belongs (Gofman's "preconsciousness") is more abstract and less well-defined. And purposely so, for as
Tindall indicates, "not multiplicity of definite mean-
ings ... but indefiniteness is the mark of the symbol."[46]
Of course, the child, like the "window" which Sologub
conceived him to be, reflects and opens out onto the
world of eternal beauty, but the exact details of this
state are left to the reader's imagination. The implica-

tions here are various: peace, harmony, goodness, eterni-
ty—all that this earthly life is not—in limitless
quantities. But because this concept itself is so broad,
it understandably defies precise definition. However, if
we accept Jung's formulation of the symbol "as the best
possible way to express something for which no verbal
concept exists ... (whose) rational component can be made
comprehensible ... (but) whose irrational component,
never to be fully explained or interpreted, can be
grasped by feelings alone,"[47] then we should willingly
expect a certain lack of precision here.

Critics have long observed Sologub's tendency toward
abstraction and generalization when portraying children.
However, although some have found justifiable fault with
this technique, few have considered it against the larger
perspective of the child's function as symbol. At the beginning of Sologub's career, Volynsky noted his "wander-
ings among abstract musings"[48] and criticized the writer
for employing unrealistic images. One of the earliest
detractors of the new currents in Russian literature, P.
Krasnov, complained that "Sologub's decadent stories ...
strike one by their strangeness of form and ... incom-
prehensibility of content."[49] And the above-cited
Volynsky, in singling out "Shadows," observes that "in
the story ... there are no figures, no characters, there
are absolutely no life-like incidents...."[50] Another
critic, directing his attention to Vanya of "The Sting of
Death," although with obvious implications for Sologub's
other child heroes, sarcastically remarks that "the
child ... reasons like a contributor to *The New Path
(Novyj put')*.... All the children of Sologub's stories
are possessed by an insane mania for death apparently
from having read too much of ... Brjusov's poetry and
Sologub's as well."[51] Gornfeld expresses similar sentiments a bit more diplomatically: "With surprising constancy Sologub portrays not children, but pre-mature
adults, adolescents, a little touched by life, a little
beyond their age; everything childlike about them is already under suspicion."[52] While there is considerable
truth to these statements, they all seem somewhat to miss
the mark by ignoring the child's essentially symbolic

Novyj put'—a journal, published in 1903 and 1904,
which largely expressed the thoughts of a group of writers and thinkers who were influenced by the idea of
Christian communalism with a marked mystical overtone.

function in Sologub's stories.   Only Modest Gofman attempted to deal with this problem when, attributing the
stiltedness of Sologub's young characters to a depiction
which is too carefully contrived, he nevertheless sought
some justification for this phenomenon.

> One cannot understand the profound work of
> Sologub without clarifying to oneself that
> *these conditions of consciousness do not have*
> *for him any subjective significance; through*
> *them he contemplates the secret reality of the*
> *world,* that which in rare moments of clairvoy-
> ance our subconscious reveals to us, this is
> the most genuine and most fundamental (con-
> sciousness) determining our entire visible
> life. This is Tjutčev's chaos, only Sologub
> infinitely more deeply studies this terribly
> complex world of secret and powerful forces,
> which for Tjutčev was still only an elementary
> element. The difference between them is that
> Tjutčev contemplates cosmic chaos, while Solo-
> gub is totally immersed in the study of the
> power of chaos in the human spirit.[53]

In deemphasizing the purely subjective significance
of the image and stressing its role as essentially a ves-
sel through which the world's secret reality is revealed,
Gofman understands that Sologub's portrayal of the child
is often meant to be less psychologically acute than met-
aphysically convincing. His function is to express symbolically a dualistic conception of the world which, like
Tiutchev's, divides life into the spheres of Cosmos and
Chaos. Yet the significant exception here is that Sologub's preconscious world ultimately points to the ordered
beauty which Tiutchev's higher reality conspicuously
lacks. On the other side of the window through which
Sologub's clairvoyant children periodically cast their
glances, absolute perfection and harmony consistently
reign, despite the different forms they may assume for
each individual character. The soothing coolness of a
star ("To the Stars"), a forest ("The Worm"), or a mountain ("The Snow Maiden"); the spell-binding enchantment
of a fairy-tale kingdom ("In Captivity," "Dream on the
Stones," "The Two Gotiks"); the bustling animation of
nature ("Earthly Back to Earth," "The White Birch")—all
of this reflects a state of soul which guarantees the

child-visionary his unique status. Martin Foss' contention that "symbolism is exact the more it succeeds in
omitting details and abstracting from everything which
could detract from the one and only route of the
whole,"[54] describes precisely Sologub's own conception of
the symbol and his consequent desire to lead his reader
unswervingly to the Platonic realm of contemplated beauty. The result of this method may indeed by an occasionally generalized and one-sided depiction of children, as
well as the often allegorical quality of Sologub's work.
But one might do well to consider Dikman's defense of the
writer's tendency toward schematization, when she claims
that "(Sologub) avoids complex thoughts, he exposes their
simple foundation, and in so doing achieves maximum ex-
pressiveness."[55]   Even Gornfeld, who felt obliged to
criticize Sologub's unrealistic portrayal of children,
recognizes the immediacy of the writer's problem and admits the simplicity and clarity with which these children
perform their function.

> (Sologub) loves his dream about children, (and)
> he wants (them) to make up for his own defi-
> ciencies; their flesh is uncorruptible, their
> blood is pure; he seeks them in his life or in
> his imagination in order to say to himself:
> there is beauty on this earth.[56]

Although heretofore we have spoken in terms of
beauty's physical existence, we should recognize that in
Sologub the child's function as symbol is to indicate not
only *where*, but also *when* beauty is found. On the latter
question Sologub's cosmogonic scheme recognizes the
sanctity of the original act of Creation in the mythical
epoch of the "beginning." It is in this period when
original beauty existed—totally, perfectly, and eternally. We need only recall Sologub's lines, "I have known
the divine supremacy / of original purity" ("Ja znal
svjatoe prevosxodstvo / Pervonačal'noj čistoty") to see
that for Sologub beauty is invariably associated with the
primordial act of creation, the initial period of man's
history. Accordingly, the further removed an object is
in time from its initial conception, from the source of
its original beauty, the more impure and unlike this
beauty it becomes. The degree to which objects, as
direct symbols, manifest—though in an imperfect and
ephemeral manner—the perfection of the original One from

which they have come, depends solely upon that object's
proximity to the time (and to the place) of this beauty's
creation. The child's appropriateness as symbol is understandable: as the being who is spatially and temporal-
ly closest to both Creator and Creation, he possesses the
primordial and perfect "essence" in the greatest amounts.

The period of childhood is seen, therefore, as a
lovely springtime when beauty, having just originated, is
in its purest state. Sologub's fascination with this
prepubescent stage of human development and with the particular consequences that accompany the loss of this
freshness through time explains his special interest in
Frank Wedekind's play, *Spring's Awakening* (1891). He
himself edited and supervised the Russian translation
(1907) and his wife reviewed it. In speaking about
Wedekind's "picture of that upheaval, of that psycho-
physical tragedy which occurs in children at the dawn of
their lives,"[57] Chebotarevskaya reveals the German writer's unquestionable influence on Sologub and expresses
attitudes certainly shared by her husband.

> The artist depicts before us the life of con-
> temporary humanity and, in a whole series of
> symbolic pictures, he embodies the first
> troubled movements of the youthful soul....
> The boys and girls portrayed in Wedekind evoke
> the deep sympathy of the reader for they are
> pure like fragrant apples. Their entire guilt
> consists of the fact that they cannot remain
> deaf and blind to the nature which surrounds
> them ... they dream about how nice it would be
> to spend the night in the forest.... They do
> not feel that they are doomed. They aren't
> aware of the fatal and horrible destiny which
> hangs over them, for this is how Wedekind de-
> scribes the awakening of sex. No writer before
> Wedekind has ever shown that the voice of sex
> rings more ominously than fate, and that spring,
> which our dramatist depicts, is a tragic
> spring.[58]

Sologub, and most probably Wedekind, must have been
aware of Schopenhauer's earlier interest in the psychosexual aspects of childhood. Nor could he have been ig-
norant of the fact that the German thinker had afforded
this crucial stage of human development a place in his

philosophical scheme, finding it appropriate to his distinction between knowing and willing:

> Just because the terrible activity of this
> [genital, S. R.] system still slumbers,
> while that of the brain already has full
> briskness, childhood is the time of innocence
> and happiness, the paradise of life, the lost
> Eden, on which we look back longingly through
> the whole remaining course of our life....
> Just because that (sexual) impulse, pregnant
> with evil, is lacking in the child, its willing
> is so moderate and is subordinated to knowing;
> and from this arises the character of innocence,
> intelligence, and reasonableness which is pe-
> culiar to the age of childhood.[59]

Sologub's interest in the child, however, transcends
Schopenhauer's limited concern with the innocent stage of
peaceful slumber. Like Wedekind, he is fascinated by the
rumblings which occur as the child awakens from his will-
less sleep and faces the frightening abyss which lies
ahead. In the German playwright Sologub found a model
not only for literarily portraying this sexual metamorphosis, but also for the tragic presentation of such
a crisis. Sologub believes as well that "tragic" adulthood destroys beautiful childlike innocence, and his
child-heroes are painfully aware of their miserable fate
all through the action of the stories. Indeed, the
"action" here often constitutes little more than the
child's recognition of pending disaster and the implications it has on his life. A plot which is constructed
around a series of continually changing events and incidents is replaced by a simple narration of a slowly un-
folding process of self-discovery, in which each child
experiences a sense of mounting fear or disgust. Besides their significance as metaphysical statements,
which argue for rejecting an evil world ruled by necessity and replacing it with a vision of life governed by
beauty and harmony, Sologub's child-centered stories contain another level of meaning. Each of them is also a
"symbolic picture" of a wonderful childlike springtime
which is doomed to annihilation by the adverse effects of
time and life. Each of them invites interpretation, as
does Wedekind's play, as psychological allegories about
the awakening of the sexual instinct in the child, his

frightened and reluctant entry into adulthood, and his
subsequent loss of innocence or withdrawal into death.

As symbol, the child leads to the abstract realm of
metaphysical thought about the nature of the universe.
On the allegorical level, he points to the intimate realm
of the psyche at a crucial stage in the personality's
psychosexual development. "All of the focus of Sologub's
poetry," Gornfeld reminds us, "is directed to the basic
problems of existence; from the very beginning, his
lyrics and stories are not only symbolic, but even allegorical."[60]   That a connection between Sologub's symbolic
stories and allegory existed in Bryusov's mind as well is
evident from his comment that "in the historical sense
(Sologub) is a symbolist. He sees symbols in everything;
he transforms everything into symbols and allegory."[61]
For those twelve and thirteen year-olds who stand at the
crossroads between blameless and "sexless" childhood and
base and sinful adulthood, it is quite clear that their
precious springlike existence is in the process of being
terminated.

Sologub's particular focus upon the internalization
of the crisis of maturation is accompanied by a certain
sluggishness of narrative pace and a mood of melancholia,
the effectiveness of which has rarely been acknowledged.
In fact, it is when read as an allegory of a soul which
currently faces the terrifying onset of sexuality that
Sologub's child-centered stories reveal their greatest
degree of power and originality. The best stories demonstrate Sologub's striking ability to convey a tone that
suitably reflects the pain and fear which the child experiences at this transitional stage in his psychosexual
development. They often brilliantly capture the confusion that ensues when he is caught in the struggle between two opposing views of himself: as an innocent,
guiltless soul who is simultaneously on the fateful brink
of a corruptive, sexual maturity. Gornfeld may be correct when he discovers that "it is impossible to say that
in (Sologub's) children there exist many different childlike images: all of them in essence are fused into one
image...."[62]   But the very impersonality and facelessness
peculiar to such allegory produces with even greater
force a disturbingly nightmarish, singularly eerie and
gruesome quality not unknown to the works of Kafka. That
critical assessment which has denigrated Sologub's stories as shapeless and lifeless was to a large extent un-
knowingly pointing to these works' greatest achievement.

For in conveying a spectral atmosphere devoid of diverse-
ly and concretely portrayed personalities, Sologub allowed a sense of free-floating fear to predominate,
thereby lifting the terror he described from a purely individual to a more general, ubiquitous level. The ultimate strength of many a child-centered story in Sologub
lies less in its success as a psychological character
study than in its effect as a mood piece.

"In the Crowd" ("V tolpe," 1907), exemplifies the
successful predominance of mood over character to produce a tedious and painfully unnerving narrative about
life's all-consuming, inescapable evil as it steadily
weighs down upon the child until it crushes him completely. From the peace and security of his home (childhood)
to the uncontrolled hostilities of an enormous crowd
(life), gathered to celebrate the seven-hundredth birth-
day of the local city, the young boy Lesha (accompanied
by his two older sisters) abandons his beauty and purity,
and travels the painful road to adulthood. As Gornfeld
wrote about this allegory:

> Perhaps the most successful of Sologub's
> stories is "In the Crowd" ... a story about
> how children cherished a sweet hope, how they
> died, crushed in a cruel, hapless, insane
> crowd, (a story) about the beastliness of life
> and a milieu where every divine feeling is
> distorted and dies, (and about) the final,
> martyred death of children.[63]

Similar to "The Worm," for example, the work relates
the continuous and frenzied build-up of external hostilities toward the boy and his sisters. This compilation
of atrocity after atrocity, where at the end there is
only exhaustion, gloom, delirium, and death, as Lesha is
unable to disentangle himself from the threatening
crowd, creates a sense of inescapable pressure which
grates on the reader as it does on the child who experiences it directly. Sologub moves from the particular
realm of the hostile crowd to the more general plane of
life itself at the end of the story, when he writes that
"the fierce blows of the devil's feet were reverberating
painfully in (Lesha's) whole body." But again like "The
Worm," "In the Crowd" can be read on another level. Not
only is the story meant to be seen from the outside in,
i.e., as an account of external forces acting against the

child, it is also intended to be viewed from the inside
out, as a story about Lesha's growing awareness of his
own inevitable entry into the world of adult values. The
story conveys a sense of private anguish and internal
confusion, invariably associated with the consciousness
of the emotional burden which the integration into adult
life places upon the uninitiated child.

The impending and inevitable integration into the
world of experience occupies the minds of all Sologub's
children —as much the older ones, such as Grishka
("Dream on the Stones"), Voldya ("Shadows") and Serezha
("To the Stars")—as their younger counterparts—Lelka
("Hide and Seek") and Paka, in the charming story "In
Captivity." Consequently, Sologub's stories are distinguished by more than the utter precision with which
they depict the threats that continually plague the child
from the outside world. These works are unique in their
revelation of the inner psychic existence of this character as he experiences the devastating pain of inevitable
personal growth. The life-death imagery which Sologub
uses in his statement that "there is no greater boundary
than that between childhood and maturity; dead people
differ from live ones no less than we adults (differ)
from children,"[64] reflects the seriousness with which he
viewed the child's emotional struggle. His gift for
translating this complex transitional state into narrative action, which is both permeated by a sustained atmosphere of fearful expectation and weighted down by a
tone of somber dread, is undeniable. The stories which
we have discussed make it abundantly clear that Sologub's
interest in the psychic world of children is inseparable
from his broader philosophical concerns. The terrible
anguish of a youngster on the border of two conflicting
psychological states transcends the exclusively personal
sphere and indicates a more general sense of ontological
malaise, which results from life's "fatal contradictions." Dikman intimates the interplay between the two
levels in Sologub's work when she claims that "philosophical reflections about the world and about man are inseparable from the spiritual world of Sologub's lyrical
hero ... and they become a personal, intimate theme."[65]
In Sologub's prose many of the concerns of the writer's
poetical "I" are transposed onto a child, and it is precisely this character in whom the intimately emotional
and abstractly metaphysical are so skillfully conjoined.

Sologub as a young child, ca. 1875.

Sologub, ca. 1890.

NOTES

[1] Unless otherwise noted, all references to Sologub's writings are taken from the *Sobranie sočinenij Fedora Sologuba v 20 tomax* (St. Petersburg: Sirin, 1913-1914).

[2] L. N. Tolstoj, *Vojna i mir* (Moscow, 1957), p. 665.

[3] For a fuller treatment of "Shadows," see Murl G. Barker, "Reality and Escape: Sologub's 'The Wall and the Shadows,'" *Slavic and East European Journal*, 4 (1972), pp. 419-426.

[4] F. M. Dostoevskij, *The Diary of a Writer* (New York: George Braziller, 1954), p. 174.

[5] D. S. Mirsky, *A History of Russian Literature* (New York: Alfred Knopf, 1949), p. 446.

[6] M. Dikman, op. cit., p. 25.

[7] D. S. Mirsky, op. cit., p. 446.

[8] R. Ivanov-Razumnik, op. cit., p. 36.

[9] F. M. Dostoevskij, *Polnoe sobranie sočinenij* (Leningrad, 1976), IV, 216.

[10] Ibid., pp. 220-221.

[11] K. Mochulsky, *Dostoevsky - His Life and Work* (Princeton: Princeton University Press, 1967), p. 615.

[12] M. Dikman, op. cit., p. 29.

[13] F. M. Dostoevskij, *Polnoe sobranie sočinenij*, XIV, 289.

[14] For an excellent discussion of Platonism in Sologub, see D. Čiževskij, "O platonizme v russkoj poèzii," *Mosty*, 11 (1965), pp. 198-205.

[15] Quoted from A. Symons, *The Symbolist Movement in Literature* (New York: E. P. Dutton, 1919), p. 17.

[16] M. Dikman, op. cit., p. 39.

[17] Nitzschean motifs are prevalent in Sologub's writing, particularly in *A Legend in Creation* and in several of the writer's dramas. An important document which makes a compelling connection between Nietzsche and Sologub is Anastasja Čebotarevskaja's "Ajsedora Dunkan v prozrenijax Fridrixa Nitčsče" (*Zolotoe runo*, 1909, No. 4, 81-83). Sologub often expressed admiration for the American dancer, and in her critique the writer's wife speaks about the importance of dance to Nietzsche's superman. She then goes on to mention overlapping themes in Sologub and Vjačeslav Ivanov. Sologub wrote a drama entitled *Nocturnal Dances (Nočnye pljaski,* 1908). For a general discussion of Nietzsche's penetration into Russia, with specific reference to Dmitrij Merežkovskij, see Bernice Glatzer Rosenthal, "Nietzsche in Russia: The Case

of Merezhkovsky," *Slavic Review*, Sept. 1974, 429-452.

[18] A. Čebotarevskaja, "Tvorimoe tvorčestvo," *Zolotoe runo*, 10 (1908), p. 58.

[19] G. Donchin, *The Influence of French Symbolism on Russian Poetry* ('S-Gravenhage: Mouton, 1958), pp. 137-138.

[20] Schopenhauer's *Die Welt als Wille und Vorstellung* (1819) appeared in a Russian translation, *Mir kak volja i predstavlenie*, in 1892. Dikman (op. cit., p. 613) cites a particularly convincing passage in Schopenhauer's work to argue the latter's influence on Sologub.

> Death is the moment of liberation from the
> monotony of individual form which does not
> comprise the secret core of our life, but
> rather constitutes a perversion of it; genuine
> freedom ensues at this moment and thus in this
> sense one can look upon it as a "restitutio in
> integrum"—a restoration to the original condi-
> tion.

James West also suggests Schopenhauer's influence on Sologub's philosophy of art, for which see his *Russian Symbolism* (London: Methuen, 1970), p. 169.

[21] F. Sologub, "Iskusstvo našix dnej," *Russkaja mysl'*, 12 (1915), 35-62.

[22] Ibid., p. 45.

[23] Ibid., p. 40.

[24] Ibid., p. 40.

[25] Mallarme's poem "Les Fenêtres" reads:

> Las du triste hôpital, et de l'encens fétide
> Qui monte en la blancheur banale res rideaux
> Vers le grand crucifix ennuyé du mur vide,
> Le moribond sournois y redresse un vieux dos,
>
> Se traîne et va, moins pour chauffer sa pourriture
> Que pour voir du soleil sur les pierres, coller
> Les poils blancs et les os de la maigre figure
> Aux fenêtres qu'un beau rayon clair veut hâler,
>
> Et la bouche, fiévreuse et d'azure bleu vorace,
> Telle, jeune, elle alla respirer son trésor,
> Une peau virginale et de jadis! encrasse
> D'un long baiser amer les tièdes carreaux d'or.
>
> Ivre, il vit, oubliant l'horreur des saintes
>   huiles,
> Les tisanes, l'horloge et le lit infligé,

La toux; et quand le soir saigne parmi les
                    tuiles,
Son oeil, à l'horizon de lumière gorgé,

Voit des galères d'or, belles comme des cygnes,
Sur un fleuve de pourpre et de parfums dormir
En berçant l'éclair fauve et riche de leurs
                    lignes
Dans un grand nonchaloir chargé de souvenir!

Ainsi, pris du dégoût de l'homme à l'âme dure
Vautré dans le bonheur, où ses seuls appétits
Mangent, et qui s'entête à chercher cette ordure
Pour l'offrir a la femme allaitant ses petits,

Je fuis et je m'accroche à toutes les croisées
D'où l'on tourne l'épaule à la vie, et, béni,
Dans leur verre, lavé d'éternelles rosées,
Que dore le matin chaste de l'Infini

Je me mire et me vois ange! et je meurs, et
                    j'aime
—Que la vitre soit l'art, soit la mysticité—
A renaître, portant mon rêve en diadème,
Au ciel antérieur où fieurit la Beauté!

Mais, hélas! Ici-bas est maître: sa nantise
Vient m'écoeurer parfois jusqu'en cet abri sûr,
Et le vomissement impur de la Bêtise
Me force a me boucher le nez devant l'azur.

Est-il moyen, ô Moi qui connais l'amertume,
D'enfoncer le cristal par le monstre insulte
Et de m'enfuir, avec mes deux ailes sans plume
—Au risque de tomber pendent l'eternité?

[26] J. West, op. cit., p. 158.

[27] "Iskusstvo našix dnej," p. 40.

[28] V. Ivanov, "Dve stixii sovremennogo simvolizma," in *Po zvezdam* (St. Petersburg, 1909), p. 248. Quoted in J. West, op. cit., p. 56.

[29] V. Ivanov, "Poèt i čern'," in *Po zvezdam*, p. 39. Quoted in V. Asmus, "Filosofia i èstetika russkogo simvolizma," in *Literaturnoe nasledstvo* 27-28 (Moscow, 1937), p. 34.

[30] Thomas Carlyle, *Sartor Resartus*. Quoted in W. Tindall, *The Literary Symbol* (Bloomington, Indiana:

Indiana University Press, 1965), p. 40. Tindall provides
neither the edition nor the page number for the Carlyle
citation.

[31] Modest Gofman, Review of F. Sologub, *Istlevajuščie
ličiny* (Moscow, 1907), *Vestnik Evropy*, 7 (1907), p. 374.

[32] A. Volynskij, *Bor'ba za idealizm* (St. Petersburg,
1900), p. 318.

[33] F. Sologub, op. cit., p. 42.

[34] F. Sologub, "Dèmony poètov," in *Sobranie sočinenij*
(St. Petersburg, 1913), 176.

[35] V. Brjusov, Review of F. Sologub, *Kniga skazok*
(Moscow, 1904), *Vesy*, 11 (1904), p. 51.

[36] V. Ivanov, *Po zvezdam*, p. 250. Quoted in J. West,
op. cit., p. 51.

[37] M. Gofman, *Kniga o russkix poètax* (St. Petersburg,
1908), p. 25. In his opening chapter, "Romantizm,
simvolizm i dekadentstvo," Gofman offers a full discussion of this topic.

[38] D. Tal'nikov, "Simvolizm ili realizm?" *Sovremennyj
mir*, 4 (1914), Part II, pp. 124-148. Quoted in West, op.
cit., p. 162.

[39] M. Dikman, op. cit., p. 17.

[40] A. Volynskij, "Novye tečenija v sovremmenoj
russkoj literature - Fedor Sologub," *Severnyj vestnik*, 12
(1896), p. 238.

[41] M. Dikman, op. cit., p. 48.

[42] Quoted in M. Dikman, p. 49. Dikman provides no
source for this statement.

[43] F. Sologub, "Ne stydno-li byt' dekadentom?" Quoted
in M. Dikman, p. 57. Dikman provides neither the place
nor the date of publication of this article, and I have
not been able to locate it.

[44] A. Volynskij, *Bor'ba za idealizm*, pp. 318-319.
Quoted by J. West, op. cit., p. 109.

[45] Samuel Coleridge, *The Statesman's Manual*. Quoted
in W. Tindall, op. cit., p. 39. Tindall provides neither
the edition nor the page number regarding the Coleridge
citation.

[46] W. Tindall, op. cit., p. 30.

[47] Ibid., p. 66. Tindall does not provide the source
of Jung's statement.

[48] A. Volynskij, "Novye tečenija," p. 348.

[49] P. Krasnov, "Russkie dekadenty," *Trud*, 11 (1895),
p. 449.

[50] A. Volynskij, op. cit., p. 236. Over the course
of time, Volynskij's attitude toward Sologub's work

changed considerably. In 1923 he published an article,
"Staryj èntuziast, F. K. Sologub" (*Žizn' iskusstva*, 1923,
no. 39), in which he praised the writer in the warmest of
tones.

[51] A. B., Review of F. Sologub, *Žalo smerti i drugie
rasskazy* (Moscow, 1904), *Mir božij*, 11 (1904), p. 118.

[52] A. Gornfel'd, op. cit., p. 57.

[53] M. Gofman, Review of *Istlevajuščie ličiny*, p. 376.

[54] Martin Foss, *Symbol and Metaphor in Modern Experience* (Lincoln, Nebraska: University of Nebraska Press,
1964), p. 10.

[55] M. Dikman, op. cit., p. 23.

[56] A. Gornfel'd, op. cit., p. 56.

[57] A. Čebotarevskaja, Review of F. Wedekind, *Probuždenie vesny* (St. Petersburg, 1907), *Russkaja mysl'*, 10
(1907), p. 196.

[58] Ibid., p. 196.

[59] A. Schopenhauer, *The World as Will and Representation*, trans. by E. J. Payne (New York:Dover, 1958), pp.
394-395.

[60] A. Gornfel'd, op. cit., p. 16.

[61] M. Dikman, op. cit., p. 49. Dikman attributes
this quotation to a note which Brjusov inscribed on the
last page of his copy of *Plamennyj krug*.

[62] A. Gornfel'd, op. cit., p. 56.

[63] Ibid., p. 55.

[64] F. Sologub, "Ljubov' i smert'," *Birževye
vedemosti*, 24, 1917, p. 6.

[65] M. Dikman, op. cit., p. 25.

CHAPTER II

FROM STORIES TO NOVELS:
THE SPECIAL CASE OF *THE PETTY DEMON*

Despite the undeniable mixture of abstract and intimate elements in Sologub's child-centered stories, it
would be inaccurate to argue the predominance of an emotional perspective in them. Nor, for that matter, do
these sketches of childhood provide a consistently satis-
factory literary portrayal of this perspective. Dikman
reminds us that Sologub is the creator of a fictional
world where "that which was earlier a state, a psychological situation, becomes a philosophical position, a
myth."[1] However, only Gornfeld's earlier notation of
Sologub's somewhat depersonalized embodiment of the child
in the short fiction suggests the imbalance which often
exists between these psychological and philosophical
positions. "It is impossible," he writes, "to say that
in (Sologub's children) there exist many different images: all of them in essence are fused into one image."[2]
And his further contention that "(the child) is not so
much a person as he is an object of fate—a necessary
conclusion of (Sologub's) conception of life,"[3] correctly
emphasizes the writer's intent to invoke the child in a
manner which resembles Ivan Karamazov's strategic presentation of children.

Only when Sologub turns to the novel—namely to *The
Petty Demon*—do we find a considerably more personal and
specifically psychological treatment of the child. Nowhere in Sologub is this figure's inner chaos better understood and more subtly depicted, nor indeed the psychological and metaphysical levels more effectively integrated, than in this book. This may partially be explained by the difference in genre, but Sologub's refusal
to delve as elaborately into the peculiar realm of the
young psyche in his other novels suggests that he is
guided here by more than formal considerations alone.
Indeed, *The Petty Demon* occupies a singular position in
Sologub's *oeuvre*. No other of his works discusses so
candidly and convincingly the philosophical tragedy which
he sees underlying the basis of life. That this same
work should contain the writer's frankest investigation
of complex youthful emotions is more than coincidental.
For Sologub's honesty about the psychological world of

children reflects, and goes hand in hand with, his openness in revealing a skeptical and disquieting vision of
reality.

Seen against the background of his predecessors in
the stories, the central child figure of *The Petty Demon*,
Sasha Pylnikov, alerts us to a critical stage in Sologub's thought and helps us to appreciate the unique quality which characterizes his most highly regarded fictional work. Most of the stories to which I have heretofore
referred were written before 1905, the year that Sologub
published *The Petty Demon* in the periodical *Questions of
Life (Voprosy Žizni)*. Up until this time, Sologub's work
reflects the writer's growing pessimism, which in many
respects *The Petty Demon*, and Sasha in particular, epitomizes. But after 1905 (and certainly by 1907, when *The
Petty Demon* appeared in a separate edition), Sologub's
writing assumes a more upbeat mood, the seeds of which
can be found already in Sasha's role in the novel. There
is, admittedly, something contradictory and ambiguous
about the child's combination of fear and faith on Sologub's part, but it is just this unsettling mixture which
constitutes the novel's special quality which I have mentioned above. *The Petty Demon*—if we cast our glance
most fixedly on its central child character—stands on
the border of two fairly distinct psycho-philosophical
states of mind in Sologub.

Of all Sologub's children, Sasha Pylinikov, the
gymnasium student who becomes the object of Ludmila's
amorous advances, is the most genuinely three-dimension-
al. His characterization exemplifies the writer's most
artistically original and psychologically sophisticated
portrayal of the confusion, ambivalence, and emotional
turmoil which typify the transition from boyhood to man-
hood. Ludmila's observation that "the best age for a boy
is fourteen-fifteen. He can still do nothing and doesn't
really understand, yet he senses everything, absolutely
everything" (250),[4] undoubtedly echoes Sologub's own
sentiments. His use of prepubescent children betrays an
enjoyment of those tense climactic moments before change
is finally affected and the transition ultimately
achieved. The frequent appearance of the child-adoles-
cent in Sologub's fiction demonstrates the author's
delectation in the perfect mixture of, and balance between, the two starkly diametrical opposites which this
unique state represents, however brief it may be. Sologub's penchant for capturing the heightened moment when

Chapter II 73

the Dostoevskian combination of psychological and metaphysical antipodes is at its peak seems best gratified
in the incipient struggle between the childlike and adult
forces within the newly-awakened youth. Sologub was not
a writer who specialized in scenes charged with dramatic
tension and excitement, yet where such moments do exist,
they are most likely to involve children. Sasha Pylnikov
represents the fullest realization of this element of
drama in Sologub's prose.

The significant interrelation of levels in *The Petty
Demon* can be appreciated when one realizes that Sasha's
movement from a condition of passive innocence to a state
of heightened sexual awareness occurs against the background of Peredonov's and Ludmila's peculiar worlds. The
specifically personal struggle within a child between
conflicting temptations toward adult sin and boyhood purity is indivisibly linked to a more general opposition
between life's vulgarity and cruelty and some transcendent ideal which must be found to counteract it. Peredonov
symbolizes the former, Ludmila and her "legend in creation" the latter. The Sasha episode of *The Petty Demon*
exemplifies Dikman's keen observance of coexisting psychological and metaphysical planes in Sologub, which we
quoted above. Indeed, in terms of the writer's use of
the child, *The Petty Demon* best realizes an objective
which Sologub would later state in his preface to the
collection of verse, *The Circle of Fire (Plamennyj krug,*
1908): "I want the intimate to become the universal."
The psychological polarities in the individual child reflect and repeat the metaphysical dualities of the world.
Sasha's internal drama, his conflict between, to use the
poet Blake's terms, innocence and experience, is exter-
nalized in the collision between Ludmila's spiritual
realm of dream, poetry, and the lyrical mood and
Peredonov's material world of banality. On a deeper
level, Sologub conceives the child's emotional disjunc-
ture as no less than the contrast between the ideal and
the real, the ability of beauty to maintain its integrity, or to exist at all, in the face of earthly powers.

The distinction between "moment" and "movement" defines the fundamental difference in Sologub's portrayal
of the central child in *The Petty Demon*. In the stories,
Sologub chooses to click the shutter, as it were, on the
precise instant of the young self's recognition of psychological transition, preferring to concentrate on the
atmosphere of fright which it induces. The ultimate

strength of many a child-centered story in Sologub lies
less in its success as a psychological character study
than in its effect as a mood piece. In *The Petty Demon*,
however, Sologub departs from this somewhat detached and
abstract approach, exemplifying rather than symbolizing
the process of "spring's awakening." Here the writer
concentrates on the *development* of character as he experiences the awareness of his own sexual maturity and as
he undergoes the conflicting emotions resulting from this
self-discovery. In switching his narrative focus onto
Sasha Pylnikov, Sologub not only presents a more human
portrait of childhood by delving into the inner workings
of the blossoming adolescent's mind; he also acknowledges
the complexity of the child's emotional world as well as
the integrity of his personality. Among the major Russian writers, only Dostoevsky before him had so exten-
sively depicted the special psychological tensions of
youth.[5] Unfortunately, V. Ilyin's suggestive observation of the connection between the two in this area,
which he made over a decade ago, has still failed to attract critical scrutiny.

> Sologub was impressed most of all by
> (Dostoevskij's) astonishing and uncanny
> details devoted to children's nightmares,
> tragedies and defects. In this sense,
> Sologub must be considered as the successor
> to Dostoevskij, who was the first both to
> reveal this new existential child's world
> and to make it the subject of great litera-
> ture.[6]

The existential world of the child, which Ilyin conjures
up, is epitomized in *The Petty Demon*. Sasha represents
Sologub's attempt to have the child function on more than
an abstract, symbolic level by assuming more complexly
human characteristics as he experiences the concrete
pain of inevitable personal growth.

In the characterization of Sasha, Sologub is concerned with a young boy's gradual maturation, marked by
a growing consciousness of his own sensuality and physical attractiveness. Sologub traverses a broad range of
sexual development in this "raw youth" from the time
that Sasha "still had never been curious to find out
whether he appeared attractive or ugly to people" (247)
until his wildly flirtatious behavior as a geisha who,

quite dexterous in sensual matters, "curtsied, lifted her
small fingers, giggled in a choked voice, waved her fan,
tapped now one man and now another on the shoulder with
it" (388). Beginning with his bashful kissing of Ludmila's elbow and proceeding to his considerably bolder
contact with other parts of her body, Sasha becomes more
deeply involved with a young woman who rouses within him
the first feelings of passion and desire. The immediate
uniqueness of this episode lies in its focusing upon the
shameless dynamics of young love. This is a subject
which Sologub had never treated before, and one which,
as we shall observe, he handles with unquestionable originality. Sologub subtly relates Sasha's discomforting
manipulation by Ludmila and his awkward engagement in
sensuous games, his bitter-sweet reactions to his blossoming sexuality, and his troubled thoughts over "impossible dreams" and "contradictory feelings." Such scenes
demonstrate a sophisticated understanding of the young
adult's psyche, years before Freudian theory had pene-
trated widely into literature. The steady transformation
of what initially are unclear stirrings and confused impulses in Sasha into more precisely and better perceived
sensual desires creates a convincing glimpse into the
world of experience.

Sasha's responses are either conveyed via internal
monologue (as in his early sense that Ludmila "came and
went ... and left only ... a vague excitement in my
soul, which is creating a sweet dream," 235) or reported
by the omniscient narrator (as is his later query: "What
is this mysteriousness of the flesh? How could he
sweetly sacrifice his blood and his body to Ludmila's
desires...?," 362). Yet in each case they reveal an
emotional condition which had not been admitted, of certainly not so clearly verbalized, in the case of Sologub's other children. To be sure, Sasha's experience
with Ludmila reveals more than Sologub's awareness of
the child's capacity for deep, complicated emotion.
Rather, the incident demonstrates an acknowledgment of
this character's *own* understanding of his serious potential as a sexual object and his ability to arouse passionate interest while himself being capable of experi-
encing desire. In this sense, Sologub expands considerably the dimensions and possibilities of literary portraiture of the child. No longer is the latter's characterization limited to a conflict-free sexuality as
observed from a removed, perspective.

Such a perspective is conspicuously present, for example, in Tolstoy's description of Nikolenka Irtenev's
inner development in *Boyhood* (1854). "But none of these
changes which had taken place in my outlook on things
struck me more than the one in which I had ceased to see
a housemaid of ours merely as a servant of the feminine
gender, and began instead to view her as a *woman*,"[7] the
narrator reflects. Nikolenka's grown-up recollection of
the time when he first notices Masha's enticing volup-
tuousness and strives to imitate his brother's sexual
advances to her is characterized by sobriety and distance. Yet precisely such qualities preclude the kind
of convincing evocation of those complicated feelings and
tense emotions, so prevalent in Sologub's depiction of a
similar psychological passage. Dostoevsky's literary
account of such a moment, "A Little Hero" (1857), also
eliminates, or at least diminishes, the sense of tortured
anxiousness and fearful confusion which accompany the
youngster's awareness of his amorous feelings toward an
older woman and his realization that his childhood has
ended. For all three writers, the incident is virtually
identical; however, Sologub's narrative technique and his
emphasis upon the sexual aspects of the maturation process signal his unarguable originality here.

William Rowe has noted that images such as the sun,
drops of water, and sweet fragrances highlight both
Dostoevsky's and Sologub's accounts of the child's emotional growth.[8] But Sologub's imagery creates a provoc-
atively sensual and suggestively erotic atmosphere which
more effectively captures the child's innermost thoughts
and desires at this stage. The frequent references to
heat which accompany the Sasha-Ludmila relationship reinforce the boy's awakening passion as he increasingly
burns with excitement in the presence of his young tempt-
ress. Ludmila's "torrid African dreams" about Sasha, her
bright, sunny room with its colorful wallpaper—all of
this creates an exotic, tropical, and seductive background, more conducive to Sasha's ripening sexuality. Her
ever-present flowers and sweet perfumes also provide a
climate of heightened sensuality which can only acceler-
ate Sasha's physical desires. Her spraying him with
fragrant scents, like the moistness of her chamber, contributes to the sticky, vaporish atmosphere, so suited to
their erotic carnal games. This spraying also recalls an
act of baptism—in this case into Ludmila's avowed religion of the flesh.

But the imagery works on yet another level. The
negative connotation of heat and fire in the novel—
Peredonov's incendiary act at the masquerade ball and
the book's epigraph, "I wished to burn her, the wicked
witch," are but a few examples—suggests the decidedly
destructive aspect of Sasha's ardent love. Ludmila loves
to sprinkle Sasha with drops of perfume, yet she also
perversely delights in the drops of Christ's blood as He
hangs from the Cross. And the same seductive charms
which lure the boy into Ludmila's world of pleasure also
hypnotize him, much as Peredonov is mesmerized by Vershina as she entices him into her luxuriant garden.
Sasha is quite the victim in his erotic escapade, rendered submissive and helpless by the very things which
have stimulated and attracted him. Thus the imagery
which Sologub employs to describe the inception of first
love implies the bitter-sweet, contradictory nature of
Sasha's private adventure while also integrating it into
the broader thematics of the novel. The unmistakably
decadent view of sex as a sweet and pleasurable experience which is nonetheless connected to decay, perversion,
and, ultimately, death, penetrates the very core of Sologub's nightmare of a once-beautiful world condemned to
corruption and banality.

On the narrative level, Sologub achieves a unique
effect in portraying Sasha Pylnikov, which, for example,
Tolstoy and Dostoevsky lack in their overly-articulate
and emotionally steady characters. Sasha's conflict is
related not necessarily through clearly verbalized utter-
ances, but rather through the recounting of his vague and
ambivalent feelings, his timid, hesitant movements, and
his often faltering speech—all of which persuasively
conveys the confusion and sense of incomprehension which
the child experiences at this crucial stage in his life.
By eliminating Tolstoy's and Dostoevsky's calm, even
tone (and we should realize that these two writers had
different objectives in mind when rendering their adolescent portraits), Sologub presents more dramatically the
sense of growing catastrophe as the distressing process
of adolescent maturation continues.

The wide variety of feelings which Sasha endures—
pain, joy, shame, exhilaration—are all the more significant because they contrast so poignantly with the dead-
ened senses of those characters who people the protagonist's lifeless realm. Sasha's personal experience seems
particularly refreshing in a loveless, feelingless world

of mechanized puppets. The merchant Tishkov thoughtless-
ly spurts his mechanical rhymes; Vershina's ward Marta
dreams about her virtues dressed as dolls; and Peredonov
himself moves slowly and apathetically like a "wound-up
doll" (289). Torturous as it is, the child's ordeal asserts the existence of natural human feelings, genuine
emotional tenderness, and the presence of concerns and
drives which are neither perverted nor destructive.
Sasha's realization of the full implications of his and
Ludmila's amorous adventures, coming on the heels of his
questions, "And what does she want?," provokes a reaction
of excited animation and free, spontaneous movement, unlike anything else in the book.

> And suddnely he blushed purple and his heart
> pounded ever so painfully. A wild ecstasy
> overcame him. He did several somersaults,
> threw himself on the floor and jumped on the
> furniture. Thousands of absurd movements
> hurled him from one corner to another, and
> his joyful, clear laughter resounded through-
> out the house (358).

Despite such happy moments, the broader dimensions
which Sasha's personality attains neither continually
evoke simple joy nor do they totally possess positive
qualities. With the onset of desire and sexual appetite
arises the problem of how this newly acquired strength
will be applied—constructively or destructively. Ludmila characteristically ignores the question when she insists that hers and Sasha's stimulations "were far from
coarse, loathsome attainments" (246). Yet, in a thoroughly Dostoevskian manner, Sologub does acknowledge that
beneath desire can lie a drive toward dominance and that
hatred as well as love can express affection. That these
contradictory tendencies extend to children, too, is seen
by Sasha's perplexed state of mind after he has been
kissed by Ludmila.

> (Ludmila's) tender kisses aroused languid,
> dreamlike thoughts. He wanted to do some-
> thing to her, pleasant or painful, tender
> or shameful—but what? To kiss her legs?
> Or beat her, long and hard, with supple,
> long twigs? So that she laugh from joy or
> cry from pain? Perhaps she desired both ...

How could he sweetly sacrifice his blood and
his body to her desires and to his shame? (362)

Sasha's momentary vacillation between the urge to
fondle or to torture recalls another literary child who
exhibits a corresponding capacity for opposing impulses
toward love and hate: Liza Kokhlakova in *The Brothers
Karamazov*. Admitting her approval of parricide and her
delight in child-suffering, the lame fifteen year-old is
more articulate and extreme about her own propensity toward evil. But as he is described in the above-cited
passage, Sasha at least shares a similar potential for
such feeling. Whether it is an expression of *Weltschmerz*
or sadism, the tendency of each toward cruelty is undeniable. In Liza's case, this cruelty comes to light in
the chapter significantly entitled "A Little Demon"
("Besonok," Bk. XI, 3) when she personally substantiates
Alesha's observation that "there are moments when people
love crime." With Sasha, the revelation occurs when, for
example, we learn that "contradictory feelings mingled in
his soul—dark and nebulous—perverse because they were
premature and sweet because they were perverse" (349).
The little demon which is seen harboring in Liza's soul
is not without its counterpart in Sasha. The predominance of conscious irony, as well as the continual use
of double entendres in Sologub's novel, make Kokovkina's
reaction to her boarder's previously mentioned exhilaration particularly meaningful. "Are you possessed or
something?" ("Čto èto ty besnueššja!" 358), she exclaims.
    In the root of the verb "besnueššja" is found the
same "bes" which characterizes Peredonov and which constitutes the book's very title. There is an implication
here that Sasha contains within himself at least the
seeds of evil, and as such he mirrors—as does Liza—the
adults, who are more central to the novel's action and
plot. This is only a hint. Yet for a moment, and a crucial moment, since it has never existed before in his
work, Sologub seems to entertain the possibility of
original sin with its terrible implication that everything in life, including the child, is, or at least is
predisposed to, evil. The point one needs to consider is
that, perhaps deliberately in this novel of occasionally
unclear or confused perspective, we are not always "com-
fortably" certain that Sasha's sinfulness is generated
solely from without. The notion that this evil may, if
only partially, come from within, that evil's presence

infers some antecedent knowledge of it (as the narrator
suggests in his remarks about the generations of Cain
who still love to kill, which precede Peredonov's murder
of Volodin), is one possible interpretation of certain
aspects of Sasha's behavior.

Thus, by suggesting Sasha's corrupt tendencies,
Sologub's analysis of the child's psyche becomes disturbingly double-edged. The novel is built on a series
of paradoxes which gradually unfold to jolt and perplex
the reader and a fundamental one is connected with Sasha
Pylnikov. The very honesty which allows Sologub to reveal the uniqueness of this personality by investigating
its complex emotions during "spring's awakening" also
serves to debunk its previously special status. The romantic fallacy of the child's unquestionable innocence
crumbles. With his inclination toward desire and enjoyment of drives heretofore dissociated from his character, a likeness to the ordinary adult is intimated.
Duality pervades everything. Upon further investigation
even the seemingly inviolable purity of childhood must
be questioned. Yet, it is precisely this discovery of
duplicity in Sasha's emotional world which signals his
full importance in the novel. The psychological crisis
of conflicting good and evil which Sologub depicts in the
individual child mirrors the metaphysical calamity which
underlies his larger vision of the world. Sologub's
newly found doubts about Sasha on the behavioral level
find their counterpart in his suspicions about life in
general on the philosophical plane, and both work hand-
in-hand in contributing to the book's pervasive sense of
nervousness and insecurity. It is here that *The Petty
Demon* illustrates Dikman's claim of the inseparability
of psychological states from metaphysical issues in Sologub's art. The intimacy which Sologub achieves in his
personalized portrait of Sasha adds credence to the more
general dimensions of his ideological argument.

Sasha's assumption of negative worldly qualities—
aggressiveness, deceptiveness, vanity—inevitably results from his continuing integration into adult life.
However, beyond its significance as an important factor
in the child's personal history, this metamorphosis contains crucial and far-reaching metaphysical implications.
The novel's pervasive sense of tragic gloom is eventually
extended to the world of children in a passage whose tone
of inevitable doom resonates with growing intensity
throughout the remainder of the work.

Only the children, tireless and eternal
vessels of God's happiness on earth, were
lively and ran and played. But sluggishness
descended even upon them, and some sort of
faceless, invisible monster, nestling behind
their shoulders, looked out now and then with
its menacing eyes on their suddenly dulled
faces (141).

Here Sologub strikes a major theme which Sasha's characterization vividly realizes. Because of the omnipresence
of a demonic energy in life, all beauty is ultimately
rendered invalid and all things, even the purest, face
gradual and inevitable extinction. This destructive
force reaches its most devastating impact when it strikes
Sasha, but it is already forecast in Ludmila's tale about
the cyclamen, "which gives pleasure and induces desires,
both sweet and shameful, and stirs up the blood" (245).
This tale is an allegory which refers specifically to
"spring's awakening" in the child. Ludmila's attribution
of three colors to the flower and the corresponding sensations which they provoke—all in order of the increasing intensity of their sensuality—actually charts the
course of Sasha's own sexual growth. That the flower's
own transformation from joy, to desire, to passionate
love, represents the extermination of childlike beauty
is verified during the remainder of the novel. Once
again, the imagery works on two levels: Ludmila's flowers
are as much "fleurs du mal" as they are fragrant blossoms
of beauty and enchantment.

References to Sasha's increasingly destructive
strength or to his unattractively "heavy, awkward hands"
(359) indicate the child's ongoing degeneration. But
nothing signals this process as blatantly as does the
symbolic scene in which Ludmila leads Sasha down into a
ravine in order to continue their amorous games. The
languid atmosphere and the specific vocabulary which
Sologub uses to convey the setting are highly suggestive.
The description of the "warm, heavy air ... (which) re-
called that which was irrevocable, (where) the sun, as if
sick, was shining dully ... in the pale, tired sky,
(where) dry leaves lay peacefully on the warm earth,
dead" (350) signals the final realization in Sasha of the
corruption to which Sologub had earlier doomed all things,
in the scene of similar coloring and tonality which we
cited above. The "irrevocable" suggests Sasha's perma-

nently lost innocence; the lifeless leaves imply the extinction of a once-blossoming plant, of Sasha-the-flower
himself—(the name "Pylnikov" is derived from the Russian
word for anther, "pyl'nik"). Images of heat and warmth,
which the writer formerly used in a positive manner, are
now exclusively negative. Significantly, it is here,
against the background of exhaustion and death, that the
child's transformation reaches its apex. Its accomplish-
ment confirms the ultimate sense of disaster which continually hangs like a pall over the novel. If "Peredonovism"—the constant slippage of all phenomena to an
intensified state of corruption and decay—represents the
major component of Sologub's philosophical vision in *The
Petty Demon*, then it is Sasha's psychological metamorphosis which demonstrates the potency of this vision.

To be sure, a story-like reading of Sasha's emotional maturation as a metaphysical allegory about the movement of all things in life toward corruption is possible.
But unique to *The Petty Demon* is the notion that ideal
childhood, the integrity of whose borders Sologub had always reverentially distinguished, itself resembles—even
if only partially—the grown-up world. Sasha's less complicated counterparts in the shorter fiction are unani-
mously terrified as their precious springlike existence
approaches its termination. Adulthood is base and sinful and these characters invariably resist it. In
Sasha's case, however, the soothingly clear distinctions
between good and evil, which the child symbolizes in the
stories, are far from firm. The portrayal of Sasha precisely in this gray area helps make *The Petty Demon*
Sologub's most disquieting work. Through a psychological
portrayal of a child who is unable to distinguish between
an exclusive like or dislike of his sexuality, Sologub
reinforces the disturbing metaphysical question of
whether the beautiful ideal can be possible at all in a
world where the absolute is lacking.

Not the least important characteristic of Sasha's
behavior is the ambivalence he exhibits toward his own
sexual awakening. His actions reveal a response to
maturity which is based not entirely on fear and remorse.
Like Ludmila, although initially cautiously and confused-
ly, he enjoys being "immersed in passionate and cruel
dreams" (356-357). Rather than avoiding or rejecting the
pangs of desire, Sasha frequently accepts them, while
displaying a willing participation in acts during which
they are satisfied. In another example of at least his

partial awareness of his emotional metamorphosis, Sasha
intuits the effect of Ludmila's perfume—"sweet but
strange, enveloping, radiantly misty, like a golden,
early, though sinful sunrise behind a white haze" (243).
The imagery here is obvious and, as in the allegory of
the cyclamen, refers to Sasha's sexual transformation.
The seeming harmlessness of the perfume's white mist
(like Sasha's own purity) belies a dangerously sensual
world of desire. Yet the child shows no resistance to
being transported by the potion's scent to Ludmila's
realm of erotic pleasure, where the new age of passion
commences. We later learn that a "shameful and passionate feeling was aroused in him" (356). However, instead
of opposing this form of initiation into the adult world,
as one might expect in a Sologub story, Sasha almost encourages it, by dreaming: "If I could fall down at her
feet as if by accident and snatch off her shoe and kiss
her lovely foot." The loss of shame and the "fall from
grace," which previously carried such categorically
harmful connotations, here contain an element of sweet-
ness. Consequently, the child's complicity in, as well
as enjoyment of, "spring's awakening" tend to put its
former implications into a new light. Indeed, whatever
the extent of Ludmila's role in Sasha's "adulteration"—
and it should not be underestimated—Sasha's own culpa-
bility would appear to place at least some of the burden
of guilt on his shoulders.

The various ambivalences, which the penetration of
the child's psyche reveals, necessarily mark a change in
regard to the Sologubian ideal which this character had
previously symbolized. To the extent that Sasha demonstrates a potential for, if not a predisposition toward
it, genuine evil may be a part of this beauty. Certainly
this hidden, unknown force may explain both Peredonov's
and Ludmila's intense curiosity toward this "mysterious
person" (236) from the very beginning. The former's interest is due to a paranoiac fear that beneath the seeming guise of a harmless student could lie a threatening
deceiver. The latter's concern is based on an erotic
urge to lead the boy to the exciting brink of sin without
his ever actually reaching it, although "herself not
noticing, Ludmila awakened in Sasha the first, albeit
still vague, manifestations of yearning and desire"
(240). Whether she understands it or not, Ludmila's
growing need to clothe the boy in different costumes implies an unnaturalness or inadequacy in Sasha which

heretofore did not exist. The ability of Sasha, by the
end of the book, to camouflage skillfully a less-than-
ideal appearance behind a mask of unspoiled innocence and
perfection suggests the alarming possibility that beneath what may seem to be the beautiful absolute could
easily lie its polar opposite.

In this sense, Sasha would appear to differ from the
children of Sologub's stories at least insofar as through
them the writer indicates the presence of a higher, flaw-
less reality. Beneath Sasha's exterior he evidently uncovers a somewhat less than perfect state. It might be
helpful to recall that Robert Maguire notes a somewhat
related reversal of roles in the novel's protagonist,
when he observes that "it is likely that Peredonov is an
unconscious parody of (Vyacheslav) Ivanov's idea of the
artist."[9] What Maguire means, of course, is that Sologub's character, far from performing the traditional
symbolist role of penetrating the higher spheres of
reality to find beauty, instead descends into the lowest
realms of life, where he envisions ugliness and baseness.
To the extent that Sasha's depiction is as contrary to
that of the customary Sologubian child as Peredonov's is
to the normal symbolist-hero, an affinity between the two
may be plausible. With its increased signs of tainted-
ness, which can be only cosmetically disguised, Sasha's
beauty is open to question. The very vocabulary Sologub
uses to convey the child's aggressive behavior, while
adorned as the geisha, seems to confirm such doubt. Two
words in the sentence "gejša, jurkaja i sil'naja, vizžala
prozritel'no, carapalas' i kusalas'" (395) ("the geisha,
nimble and strong, was screaming piercingly and scratch-
ing and biting")—"jurkaja" and "vizžala"—have been used
previously to describe the quintessence of *Peredonovism*,
the nasty and foul *nedotykomka*. One might actually argue
that Sasha's gradual but inevitable sexual maturity
serves as a thematic counterpart to Peredonov's increasing acts of vileness and destruction. The process of
each runs as two parallel lines which finally intersect
during the masquerade. Here Sasha's gradual "adulteration" enters a more advanced stage when he convincingly
acts the role of the geisha, much as Peredonov's destructiveness reaches new heights when he sets fire to the
club and prepares to murder Volodin.

Sasha's aunt does not necessarily admit to any
change in her nephew's beauty even though she remarks,
ironically, that "he is exactly the same child as he was,

or is he so spoiled that he is deceiving (me) even by his face?" (400). However, her doubt meaningfully reinforces the schoolmaster Khripach's wise observation that "appearances are sometimes deceptive" (200). This remark plants an inescapable note of suspicion in the reader's mind about any final determination about the characters. Whether recognized or not by Sasha's aunt, the mere suggestion of the possible illusiveness of the absolute, the implication that the seeds of evil may be contained within and nurtured by beauty itself, seriously challenge the existence of any redemptive ideal or absolute harmoniousness.

As the major figure to intimate the deceptiveness of a previously assured incarnation of innocence, Sasha indicates the lack of fixity and uncertainty which pervade Sologub's world view. He is the character who most unambiguously establishes the importance of the theme of reality and illusion, which is first sounded in the novel's opening paragraph and then reverberates throughout: "It seemed that everyone lived peacefully and amicably in this town. And even happily. But it only seemed that way" (37). Sasha's characterization strikes at the very core of the narrative tone and overriding philosophy of *The Petty Demon*. This instability extends to the stylistic level of the book, whose dual-leveled imagery, double entendres, and numerous puns signal a breakdown in communication itself; words no longer relay unqualified meaning. The depiction of Sasha reflects the nervous interplay and deep-seated ambiguity which exist between the demonic powers of destruction and the "dionysian" forces of ecstasy and inspiration continually at work in the novel. In this sense the Sasha episode may be considered to represent the structural and philosophical center of *The Petty Demon*. Both Peredonov and Ludmila need Sasha, both vie for control of him, in order to prove the predominance of their respective world views. Through him, Peredonov attempts to demonstrate that all must be dragged down into the mire, while Ludmila tries to establish that in order to have beauty man need only create it.

Sasha's transformation surely gives some credence to Peredonov's suspicions, if not to his extreme reactions: evil does threaten everything, even the absolute of beauty. In its own way, the child's metamorphosis questions just how "mad" Peredonov actually is, as does Ludmila's observation that "only in madness is there

happiness and wisdom" (361). But more importantly,
Sasha's characterization challenges the absolute validity
of beauty itself. Indeed, through this figure the
writer finds that truth and beauty are not necessarily
the same. The child serves as a persuasive example of
the applicability of a Peredonov-oriented ideology, which
insists that a world ruled by necessity is artificial,
false, and ultimately corrupting. In this sense, Sasha
reflects Sologub's greatest fears, and of all the writer's literary children, he seemingly constitutes the
epitome of his negative philosophical vision.

However, in questioning the absolute integrity of
the ideal, Sologub, through the character of Sasha, in no
way argues that man can exist without it. Sasha is also
the central focus of Ludmila's dream, and as such he
shows that her illusory vision of beauty is still purer
than Peredonov's mundane and vulgar reality. Her corruption is less harmful than his deliberate destruction of
the boy. Sologub manipulates Sasha in *The Petty Demon* to
prove that although beauty must inevitably be soiled by
the evil inherent in man, paradoxically—and tragically—
man needs the very thing which he himself destroys. It
is true that when Ludmila corrupts her ideal she complies
with the world as it necessarily is and thereby substantiates its power. But her stubborn insistence in believing nevertheless in the inviolability of Sasha's
beauty demonstrates a faith and an individual will which
are even stronger and more compelling than the "truth."
So important is Ludmila's need to love a beautiful image
of Sasha that she believes in the child despite the
change which she helps to effect in him. And here is
where Sasha indicates a new dimension in Sologub's work.

Ludmila's incarnation of the ideal in the person of
the child mirrors nothing less than Sologub's similar
practice in his fiction. Through her, the writer re-
states a Dostoevskian belief that "beauty will save the
world," not so much because it is truthful, but rather
because it is the touchstone of a faith without which
man's vision would be hopelessly bleak and his individual
will totally powerless. "If the entire world lies in the
bonds of necessity, then what of my freedom which I also
feel as a necessary law of existence?," Sologub would
later ask in his essay "The Art of Our Day." "Our [gen-
eration's, S.R.] individualism was not a rebellion
against social mindedness, but a revolt against mechanical necessity, against an excessively materialistic world

view."[10]   The writer might have easily been talking about
Ludmila as well. For on its most vital philosophical
level, *The Petty Demon* rehearses the struggle for faith
in light of a nightmarish vision of reality which does
everything to disprove it. Insofar as the object of this
faith is itself ambiguous in *The Petty Demon*, we might
infer that Sologub believed it could be gained, to use
Dostoevsky's words, "only through the crucible of
doubts." If this is the case, then Sasha fulfills his
function perfectly.

Sasha Pylnikov ultimately suggests a need for faithfulness to an ideal of beauty, the loyalty to which
transcends the truthfulness of this beauty. As such, the
boy's characterization reflects Sologub's agreement with
Dostoevsky's feelings about his ideal, namely that "even
if it were proved to me that Christ was outside the
truth, I would still prefer to remain with Christ than
with the truth."[11]   Yet having said this, we must
acknowledge that the portrayal of Sasha represents a
fictively demonstrated "proof" which Sologub would never
again allow himself to repeat. As we shall see, in his
next novel, the trilogy *A Legend in Creation*, he returns
to his "abstract musings" by rendering his most symbolic
child portraits of all: the hero's mysterious son,
Kirsha, and the eerie, supernatural "quiet children."

* * * *

Even with its greater psychological emphasis, *The
Petty Demon* still demonstrates that beyond Sologub's desire to uncover the dynamics of pubescence lay an interest in expressing his objection to the prevailing values
and attitudes of the contemporary materialistic age.
Dikman stresses this phenomenon when, after careful
study of Sologub's literary opus, she finds that "for
Sologub, children's suffering exposes the trouble and
abnormality of life."[12]   The presentation of Sasha in
particular substantiates Peter Coveney's claim in his
far-reaching study of the literary treatment of children
in nineteenth and twentieth century England, namely, that
"the child could serve as symbol of the artist's dissatisfaction with the society which was in the process of
such harsh development around him."[13]   Sasha's unique structural position in *The Petty
Demon*, as the person whose fate the two major characters
vie to control, evidences Sologub's condemnation of

certain contemporary social and ideological outlooks. As
the quintessential representative of a society where respect is gained solely by rise in position and power and
where interest in higher spiritual values is all but
gone, the emblematic Peredonov exhibits his greatest
and most characteristic evil when he abuses children
and denies the child in others. To the person who considers the ultimate achievement in life to be his treas-
ured inspectorship, any absence of the all-pervasive cor-
ruptiveness of this world or any trace of the intangibly
nonearthly is deemed threatening and unnecessary.
Peredonov's malicious teasing of the pleasant Misha
Kudryavtsev; his bullying of the harmless Kramarenko,
the innocent Antosha Gudaevsky, and the defenseless
brother of Marta, Vladya; and finally, his unceasing
torment of Sasha Pylnikov himself are, in fact, but individual examples of society's more widespread and even
fiercer hostility toward any form of beauty whatsoever.

But Sologub's primary intent in the novel is to
attack not his age, as would some civic writer, but
rather the evilness of life in general, at all times and
in all places. This is best evidenced at the costume
ball, where the masqueraders become a metaphor for life
itself. Here the crowd's perpetuation of collective
evil against the geisha, as it symbolically destroys the
unique beauty which she represents, validates one of the
narrator's saddest admissions and most bitter commentaries, that "truly in our age it is beauty's lot to be
tainted and violated" (102). Sasha's function in this
scene, as well as in the novel at large, is to suggest,
recalling the argument, if not the apocalyptic overtones
present in Dostoevsky's *The Idiot* and *The Possessed*, that
in a world where the concept of beauty is absent or de-
filed, man is reduced to a beast and is doomed to inevitable disaster. Beauty's place is preserved—and by
extension, spiritual transformation is assured—only when
man ignores the petty concerns of everyday life and re-
serves a place for the adoration of the nonmaterial.
Ludmila's appreciation—indeed, idolatry—of an ideal
perfection, ephemeral and decadent though it may be,
signifies a joyous diversion and ecstatic escape from
vulgar and demeaning "bestial life" *"zverinyj byt."*[14]
By disregarding (as Peredonov cannot) the phenomenal
realm of foul nature and ugly matter, which she does for
example during her walk with Sasha to the ravine, Ludmila

seems to negate, or at least to undermine, its ultimate
importance.

NOTES

[1] M. Dikman, op. cit., p. 27.
[2] A. Gornfel'd, op. cit., p. 56.
[3] Ibid.
[4] All quotations from *The Petty Demon* are taken from
the 1933 edition (Moscow-Leningrad: Academia), reprinted
by Bradda Books (Letchworth: Hertfordshire), 1966.
[5] Čexov was also interested in child psychology, although the overall role of this character in his fiction
is not as extensive as it is in Dostoevskij's or Sologub's writing. For an informative survey on this topic
in Čexov, see Ju. Ajxenval'd, "Deti u Čexova," in
Siluèty russkix pisatelej, Vol. II (Moscow, 1917), pp.
211-226.
[6] V. Il'jin, "Fedor Sologub 'Nedobryj' i zaga-
dočnyj," *Vozroždenie*, 158 (1965), p. 61.
[7] L. N. Tolstoj, *Sobranie sočinenij v 20 tomax*
(Moscow, 1960), I 143.
[8] W. Rowe, *Doestoevsky: Child and Man in His Works*
(New York: New York University Press, 1965), p. 71.
[9] Robert Maguire, "Macrocosm or Microcosm? The Symbolists on Russia," in *Russia: The Spirit of Nationalism* (New York: St. John's University Press, 1972), p.
133.
[10] "Iskusstvo našix dnej," p. 44.
[11] F. M. Dostoevskij, Letter to N. D. Fonvizin, March,
1854. Quoted in Letters of *Fyodor Michailovich Dostoevsky*, trans. by E. C. Mayne (New York: Horizon Press,
1961), p. 71.
[12] M. Dikman, op. cit., p. 32.
[13] Peter Coveney, *Poor Monkey* (London: Rockliff,
1957), p. ix.
[14] Sologub frequently uses this phrase in his writings to signify the polar opposite of his desired "living life." In the longest of his stories "A Bestial
Life" ("Zverinyj byt," 1912), Sologub depicts the struggle of the hero, Kurganov, to rescue his twelve year-old
son from the corruptive influence of Petersburg, "a contemporary Sodom," and escape with him to the peaceful,
purifying countryside.

CHAPTER III

THE NOVELS: THE CHILD AND ADULT

Although the figure of the positive child functions
similarly to underscore the lack of aesthetic sensitivity and spiritual awareness in society, one needs to distinguish a basic difference in his role in Sologub's
shorter and longer works. Whereas in the stories Sologub
uses the child essentially to establish the existence of
some transcendent value or higher reality, in the novels
he employs this character largely to deal with the problem of whether, and how, man can reach this special state
and transcend himself. To put it differently, if in the
stories the figure of the child guarantees the location
of the all-important ideal and confirms it as an essential part of man's consciousness, then in the novels his
presence raises the question of whether the ideal may be
attained in life and, if so, at what cost. In his sub-
sidiary role in the novels, the child appears as a foil
for the protagonist's actions, as a sounding board for
his ideas about himself and about the world. Furthermore, Sologub's special children point to some significant patterns, for in *Bad Dreams, The Petty Demon,* and
A Legend in Creation they represent the ideal which each
positive hero or heroine is seeking and often lead the
latter directly to it. The child provides the novels'
protagonists with some form of diversion from the humdrum routine of their lives or from the dissatisfaction
they feel with themselves. He is associated with
Login's, Ludmila's, Trirodov's, and Ortruda's attempts
to escape the reality which is everywhere stifling and
hostile, and to substitute in its place a more attractive existence. And in *Sweeter Than Poison* the pattern
is different only because here it is the child herself
who, at least initially, is engaged in an activity customarily reserved for an adult. The heroine Shanya's
love of Zhenya, which is traced from its earliest stages
(when the girl is fourteen) to its final ones (when she
reaches adulthood), provides a similar means of diversion in *Sweeter Than Poison,* as does the protagonists'
involvement with children in Sologub's other novels.

A discussion of the different forms which this escape assumes, as well as the various portrayals of the
children who are related to it, is important not only for

understanding the individual work in question. Traced
from novel to novel, the writer's depiction of children
and the particular kinds of escape they indicate, reflect
Sologub's philosophical and stylistic evolution and the
ultimate triumph of his "struggle for idealism." The
young boys, Tolya and Lenya, are connected to the hero's
anti-urban ideal in Sologub's first novel, *Bad Dreams*,
where the traces of naturalism are strongest in the writer. The more elaborately depicted Sasha of *The Petty
Demon* reflects a rather balanced mixture in Sologub of
realist and symbolist elements. The mysterious quiet
children in *A Legend in Creation* are examples of the
writer's cosmic symbolism and they represent, as does
the novel in which they appear, Sologub's closest approach to the "fantastic" as a fictive genre. More so
than in his stories, the children in Sologub's novels
reveal the most fundamental rhythms of the writer's pre-
World War I literary development.

Particularly because they emphatically betray the
writer's artistic and spiritual development, it is surprising that Sologub's novels have suffered such critical neglect. That this genre holds a special place in
his *oeuvre* is substantiated at the very least by their
conformation to a distinct pattern, part of which I have
mentioned above. *Sweeter Than Poison* and *The Charmer of
Snakes* are excluded from this pattern for their own
specific reasons. A substantial portion of the loosely
constructed *Sweeter Than Poison* was originally published
as a long story and consequently this extension of an
earlier work was not an organically conceived novel.
Lacking any important child-characters, *The Snake Charmer* was written after the Bolshevik Revolution and therefore has no immediate tie to the most substantial, decadent-symbolist   phase of Sologub's career. But the
five major novels, *Bad Dreams*, *The Petty Demon*, and the
trilogy, *A Legend in Creation* may be seen to a large degree—as they were by many contemporary critics—as con-
stituting a single tapestry. In addition to similarities already noted, the central male protagonist in each
is a schoolteacher, reflecting Sologub's own experience
until his retirement from the educational profession in
1907. Indeed, it is an arresting fact of Sologub's literary biography that the eight-year period (1884-1892)
during which time he served as a provincial schoolteacher
inspired the setting, as well as most of the characters
and situations of all his novels.[1]

Of course, Sologub's novels contain a greater variety of children than has thus far been conceded. Not all
of these characters are charged with the special value of
which we have been speaking, although those who lack it
make only cameo appearances. Interest, then, in the
"negative" Sologubian child—the one who participates
fully in the world of experience—is obviously not based
on his individual performance, since his connection to
the given work's action or plot tends to be exceedingly
brief and inconsequential. Rather, the significance of
these negative children lies in their persistent appearance throughout each phase of Sologub's career. Their
characterization indicates the continual presence of
realist or naturalist elements in Sologub's fiction and
the writer's on-going faithfulness to many of their
tenets. As we shall see, no Sologubian novel belongs
completely to any one school. The early *Bad Dreams* in
some respects qualifies as a naturalist piece of fiction.
The later *A Legend in Creation* was written when the symbolist strain in Sologub's fiction was extremely strong,
yet the work exhibits features which are traditionally
not associated with such a style of writing. Sologub's
novels show, to quote Harry Levin's finding of a somewhat similar phenomenon in James Joyce, that "it is possible for a writer to be rich and copious in his words,
and at the same time to give the reality, which is the
root of all poetry, in a comprehensive and natural form.[2]
This is not the place to embark upon a detailed discussion of the post-realist trend in European and Russian
fiction of the 1870s and 1880s which historians of literature have termed "naturalism."[3] But by imitating the
crude behavior of the adult milieu from which they come
and by helping to reflect the lower, less edifying aspects of human existence, which are depicted in each of
Sologub's novels, the negative children do reveal the
writer's appreciation of some techniques and practices of
this literary school. The behavior of these characters
is frequently brutish, highlighting, as, for instance,
Zola's naturalism tends to do, man's basically animal-
like nature. They also help to convey the overall sense
of moral and physical degeneration in a world devoid of
positive ideals or values. Removed from any psychological consideration, the portraiture of these children
demonstrates an appalled focus on unredeemed social and
physical data. A literary technique which emphasizes
the exposure of social evils rather than the penetration

of human emotions is transparent in Sologub's treatment
of the most important of these negative children.

Petka Motovilov, the repellent son of the corrupt
school official in *Bad Dreams*, who has "rotten teeth, a
greenish face, a driveling smile, a sunken chest (and)
unleashed interest in younger girls" (II, 152), epitomizes the dissolution of family life and the lack of a
nucleus in which warm human relationships can be expressed or developed. His elder sister Nata's incessant
coughing and spitting of blood is symptomatic of the
disease which has run rampant in the town and which
threatens to destroy or incapacitate larger segments of
the populace. The court investigator Ukhanov's claim
that "even the children that (Motovilov) has are degen-
erates" (I, 224), is especially significant because the
attention it calls to hereditary factors at work in the
family of this "habitual criminal" is characteristic of
a major area of concern for the naturalists. The schoolteacher Valya's pupils, "amazing little beasts with
filthy paws and unwiped noses (who) were obtuse and ig-
norant" (II, 209), emphasize the state of barbarity and
neglect which is the order of the day. Although these
children represent only a part of the picture of stultifying provincial life depicted in the novel, they nevertheless serve both to alert the reader to the serious
proportions of this decay as well as to enhance the
claustrophobic effect which Sologub creates in his vision of a world helplessly entrenched in the mire of its
own sordidness.

The depiction of a hermetically-sealed universe,
dominated by corruption and vice, is a primary structural
and philosophical concern in *The Petty Demon* as well.
The nightmare of a world in which evil is all-pervasive
is largely substantiated by the many children in the
novel who mirror the offensive traits so prevalent in
their depraved elders. Along these lines one could cite
the self-satisfied Vitkevich, whose lust for women and
desire to marry Vershina in order to obtain a better
position recall the protagonist's own behavior. Or, we
remember the mischievous Avdeev boys, whose malicious
act of smearing tar on the gates of Marta's house resembles the destructive and spiteful behavior of
Peredonov's circle. The crude actions of these figures
help to convey life's seamier side and they represent a
deployment of children which, except for "The Sting of
Death," is generally absent in Sologub's stories. Those

whose characterization most firmly establishes the serious extent of the corruptedness of the social milieu are
Grushina's children, "ragged, dirty, stupid and evil,
like scalded puppies" (75). Their shabby clothing, their
vulgar use of foul language, and their obscene gestures
not only place them squarely in the unattractive landscape against which the action unfolds, but also reinforce the narrator's worst fears of that "faceless monster," which uncontrollably debases everything in its
path.

A *Legend in Creation*, the writer's most experimental
and fantastic work, continues to relate the features of
gloomy, mundane reality with considerable specificity.
Merely to note the presence of the reactionary Kerbakh's
lisping son, who is bullied into assuming the most taste-
less human prejudices, is sufficient to call attention to
the book's opening charge about life's coarseness and
ugliness, which the negative child himself duly represents. The boy's description as "a little eight year-
old, dribbling and black-toothed" (XVIII, 66), contains
the traditional stock epithets reserved for Sologub's
evil children, and once again it focuses attention on
physical and social, as opposed to psychological detail.

The above-cited negative children, whose presentation indicates at least some traces of naturalism in
Sologub's writings, are no less "cosmic" in their implication of a terrible, ubiquitous evil than the writer's
positive children, who symbolize the existence of a higher beauty in life. These evil children emphasize the
growing momentum of the forces of deterioration which are
unmistakably at work in Sologub's novels. Exemplifying
the pattern which informs the novels under consideration,
each work gradually moves toward a final catastrophe,
which the reader has sensed all along. Each book ends
with an act of destructiveness and collective violence,
even as the idealist protagonist seemingly triumphs. The
end of *Bad Dreams* relates the riot which takes place in
the town as rampant crowds storm Login's house. In *The
Petty Demon* chaos reigns at the masquerade while the hall
goes up in flames. On the final pages of A *Legend in
Creation*, Trirodov and his entourage barely escape in
their balloon as scores of angry townsfolk arrive to destroy his colony. The point here is that Sologub's portrayal of children who duplicate their corrupted elders
is part of a larger trend in his novels: the presence of
a scientific determinism which lies beyond the control of

individuals and guarantees the perpetuation of human
beasts. Sologub demonstrates how individuals are forced
to submit to laws—social, physical, and biological—
which operate outside of them. And such a situation produces the fundamental tension of the writer's novels: a
world of determinism and necessity is confronted by a
self-willed individual who attempts to establish his
freedom and create his own laws. Naturalism, of course,
was inspired more by science than by art. No wonder,
then, that Sologub's final and most "complete" hero,
Trirodov, is both a poet and a chemist: in *A Legend in
Creation* the feud, as it were, between naturalist and
symbolist ideologies is at its fiercest with the latter,
predictably, triumphing in the end.

Sologub's frequently elaborate description of the
minutiae of every-day life and particularly of its negative qualities, has enticed some critics to single him
out as a naturalist among his symbolist contemporaries.
With its general lack of concentration on psychological
portraiture, which is more characteristic of realism, and
with its obvious lack of sympathy toward the milieu which
is depicted, the writer's work contains, according to
Dikman, a singularly "naturalistic nakedness (obnaženn-
nost')."[4] This same critic is led to observe, echoing
Bryusov's earlier cited comment (p. 53) about Sologub's
organic ties to the earth, that "Sologub's decadence is
not the cerebral philosophy of Minsky* or the refinement
of Z. Gippius; (for) behind it stands the tormenting,
socially-typical experience of life."[5] The children of
Sologub's novels further demonstrate what their counterparts in his stories earlier revealed: that the poet who
was capable of abstract musings and idealistic flights
was also a writer who showed a keen interest in the con-
ditions of the here-and-now.

"No, you won't erase Sologub from Russian reality,"
Bely had reminded a public which by-and-large ignored
Sologub's realism. "He is tied to it with (his) flesh
and blood."[6] The peculiar and undoubtedly contradictory
combination of the distant and the local, of the exalted
heights and the lower depths, provided the critic Gornfeld with sufficient ammunition to dispute the widespread

*Pseudonym for N. M. Vilenkin (1855-1937), poet and
philosopher and one of the earliest Russian symbolists.
It was Minsky, incidentally, who recommended that the
writer change his name from Teternikov to Sologub.

claim about Sologub's alleged estrangement from life, to
which Bely was also responding. He defended his place as
fitting squarely in the Russian "civic" tradition when he
argued that "Sologub does not constitute a break with the
Russian element, but on the contrary, urban Russia, Russia of the middle class and the upstart intelligentsia
and Russia of the streets, has found in him a spokesman.
He is not only the most genuine decadent among the Rus-
sians, but is also the most Russian among the decadents."[7]

It is entirely predictable then that Sologub's first
novel, published serially in 1895, but begun as early as
1883, should contain the strongest civic influence and
betray the heaviest dose of the Russian reality which
Bely mentions. *Bad Dreams* abounds in detailed descriptions of people's dress and personal characteristics, as
well as the town's dirty streets and corrupt institutions.[8] Yet, because the carefully depicted natural and
social milieux serve primarily as background for Sologub's more immediate investigation of the soul of his
central protagonist, *Bad Dreams* transcends the restricted
goals of naturalism and betrays a realist influence.
Here I have in mind the criterion which Donald Fanger
uses to distinguish Dostoevsky's works from the tradition which had played so significant a role in his literary development. And when one replaces "city" with
"province," Fanger's statement could easily apply to
Sologub's novels.

> (Dostoevsky) presented for the first time the
> life of the city in all its sordidness - not
> simply to show what these conditions automat-
> ically did to people, as the naturalists would
> show, but to raise the problem of how, within
> them, sentient human beings might pursue the
> quest for human dignity.[9]

Not unlike his Dostoevskian counterpart, Raskolnikov, Sologub's hero, the thirty year-old schoolteacher,
Vasily Markovich Login, is obsessively preoccupied with
the idea of transcending the oppressive drabness of his
physical reality as well as a self conception which insists that he can be spiritually no better than he currently is. To use Fanger's words about Dostoevsky's
protagonist, Login is also in the process of pursuing
"the quest for human dignity." Continually throughout

the novel, Login expresses a desire to achieve an ideal
state which will liberate him from the feelings of
weariness, hostility, and sinfulness which he has about
himself and the world. Login's world is one of stifling
provinciality, gross hypocrisy, and crass officialdom,
from which—beginning with the book's very first page—
he feels removed and alienated. His initial refusal to
participate with the other guests in the ongoing card
game signals his determination to resist conforming to
the routine trivialities and demands of his everyday existence. His growing awareness of his inability and lack
of desire to fit into society's mainstream qualify Login
for inclusion into the pantheon of superfluous men who
populate the pages of nineteenth century Russian literature. In fact, one of the novel's few sympathetic characters, Anna's father, Yermolin, calls Login superfluous
quite early in the novel, in Chapter Three. Thus, Sologub presents his hero in the first scene as standing off
by himself and quite fatigued at the Kulchitsky party,
much as Dostoevsky emphasizes Raskolnikov's solitude as
the latter, in the opening paragraph, emerges from his
room, which symbolizes his apartness from the teeming
world which surrounds him.

References to *Crime and Punishment* are, incidentally,
not gratuitous here, for Dostoevsky's novel served as the
major model for Sologub's own first attempt in this
genre. The similarities between the books' two heroes
are great indeed. Both are brooding, solitary intellec-
tuals who are also capable of spontaneous feelings of
generosity and love. Both commit murder as an act of
protest, specifically a murder of an older person, who
symbolizes the worst aspects of the society which the
hero despises. Both are in love with a young woman, who
represents the purest elements of life and who, in each
case, leads the hero to the promised salvation, which is
mentioned at the end of the books. For example, can not
one imagine Raskolnikov, during his several visits with
Sonya, uttering or thinking Login's exact words about
Anna?: "What do I, who am immoral, have in common with
her, who is chaste? It is such torment to be with her
nowadays: a hopeless wandering by the locked doors of a
lost paradise!" (II, 301)

"I will once again tear myself away from this swamp
so that I myself do not become a total beast and completely lose my human image,"[10] the author had written to
a friend while working on the novel, fully echoing the

sentiments of his future hero. Sologub's portrayal of
Login is geared almost exclusively to showing the degree
of his sentience—although by no means undermining his
capacity for lewdness. Login's path toward human dignity
is certainly not without its detours, and his behavior
often contradicts the very purity and idealism of his
positive vision. He conducts erotic escapades, engages
in often perverse fantasies, commits murder, and constantly throughout the novel denigrates himself. A disen-
chanted idealist, as his friend Andozersky calls him,
Login recognizes the fruitlessness of his ideal not only
because of the hopelessly backward and barbaric society
which surrounds him but also because of the defects in
his own character and behavior. Whether his glance is
cast inward or outward, he sees mostly darkness. But in
those important moments when he does see bright spots,
they are often in the form of certain fragmentary youthful recollections or of visions of the two positive children in the novel, Tolya and Lenya. It is a testament to
his central role in the novel that the child reveals precisely the protagonist's wavering between the positive
impulses of his idealism and the negative urges of his
sinfulness. Take, for example, the incidents in Chapter
Twenty where Login first feels a strong homosexual attraction to young Lenya's naked body and then enjoys the
thought of cruelly beating it. These moments demonstrate
the child's part in determining the degree of the hero's
pervertedness and the extent to which it separates him
from his ideal of moral purity. Yet it is Login's positive goal of self-transcendence which is emphasized in
the novel, and the same child character serves as a major
focal point of his search to overcome the dreary tedium
of his existence and to regain his "human image." So it
is not, then, as individual personalities, certainly to
the degree that Sasha Pylnikov is one, that the book's
positive children—Tolya, the heroine's brother, and
Lenya, the orphan whom Login adopts—are noteworthy.
They are portrayed largely as set static types, with
recognizable romantic overtones. It is rather the kind
of detail that Sologub uses to describe the children, the
particular settings in which they are placed, and the response which they elicit from the hero, which ultimately
determine their significance.

    From the very beginning, and continually thereafter,
the child is connected to the most dynamic element in
Sologub's fiction, to a theme which one can broadly label

as escape. Insofar as this goal constitutes the major
concern of most of Sologub's protagonists, the child's
ancillary status in no way compromises his crucial position in the novel at large. Although positive children
are used less in *Bad Dreams* than in Sologub's other novels,
their appearance nevertheless signals a radical shift in
mood and an important change in emphasis for the hero and
for the reader, who is always privy to the forces which
are responsible for the latter's personal crisis. Physi-
cally, these characters are most often set apart from the
locale of the novel's dominant action; each is associated
with an upliftingly pastoral setting of light, fresh air,
lush vegetation, and fragrant aromas. Whether they show
the child playing in the grass, fishing, or resting in a
forest clearing, these outdoor scenes stand as fixed
pieces, genre paintings wherein physical description permanently captures a moment of serene beauty and literary
style exhibits a distinctly poetic diction. Here, as
elsewhere in Sologub's novels, the positive child marks a
rejection of life's darker sides in favor of a more lyrical element, the specific qualities of which clarify the
hero's strivings, as well as the writer's own philosophical orientation. Login's perception of these lyrical in-
terludes—and they occur, significantly, only in his
presence—precipitates a turning point in emotional tonality: melancholy and boredom change to joy and excitement. For example, in the passage which describes
Login's first encounter with Tolya and his sister Anna
Ermolina, the hero's future beloved, the somberness,
sluggishness, and general gloominess which constitute the
predominant tone and atmosphere of the novel, completely
disappear.

> The boy was talking to Anna and smiling. The
> bright peak of his gray-white cap, which was
> handsomely turned upwards, disclosed his dark
> face. Illumined by the sun, diminished by the
> distance, and seen clearly through Login's
> glasses, as if he were etched in fine distinct
> lines, he appeared bright, as if he were in a
> picture which had a background of a blue river
> and bright verdure. His white blouse was drawn
> together by a polished dark belt with a small
> clasp. At times Anatolij would come out of the
> water and climb onto one of the rocks on the
> shore (II, 28).

The colors here are bright and there is an abundance of words which connote cleanliness and radiance.
The sun's influence is positive; it warms rather than
parches, as it often does in the novel. The river is
clear blue and the vegetation is a healthy bright green.
The child and his ambience signal a rare state of whole-
someness in a society which chronically suffers from a
disease that mushrooms to epidemic proportions by the
end of the novel. His very presence in *Bad Dreams* suggests that redemption can be found in the values which
this character comes to represent.

One of the basic functions of the child, or more
broadly speaking, childhood, since in the novels Sologub
often moves from observations of individual children to
statements about the childhood state in general, is to
awaken the hero's nostalgia for the innocent joys of his
past. Children help return Login to the idealism of his
youth and allow him to hope for redemption from what he
considers to be the burden of his adult present. "How
inexpressibly good it would be," he exclaims, "to grow
little, to become a child, to live on impulse - and not
to ponder over life" (II, 197).

Bad Dreams is the novel of Sologub in which the hero
most often casts his gaze backward, and as such the book
most faithfully captures the overriding spirit of the
1880s. Then, if one is to believe such literary spokesmen of the decade as Nadson and Garshin, or the cultural
historian Ivanov - Razumnik,[11] the dominant mood was one
of hopelessness and frustration, which could not help but
he contrasted to, and indeed aggravated by, the remembrance of a former time of bright ideals and hopes. "In
this nervous age," Login confesses to his friend Claudia,
"no one has the strength to accomplish anything. With
the temperament of a disillusioned frog, how can we go in
for adventures?" (II, 81) Login's habit of measuring the
failure of his present life in terms of its distance
from a period of wholeness and purposefulness recalls
several of Chekhov's characters in the 1880s. Figures
such as Ivanov and the professor in "A Boring Story" are
also miserable because their formerly positive self-
images are no longer able to sustain them. In *Bad
Dreams*, however, the child reminds the hero of his happy
past, and also inspires him to believe that he can recapture and relive this state. "A modern man, living
more through bookish and abstract interests, having lost
the old laws of life, tired, enfeebled, sinful, Login

seeks the truth...,"[12] Sologub had written about his protagonist, implying a need for an antidote to his condition, which the children in the novel will purvey.

That Login is periodically able to see childhood
qualities in his own self, specifically when observing
Tolya and Lenya, speaks to one of the child's fundamental
roles in the book. For just as on the physical level the
child testifies to the existence of genuine beauty amid
the world's sordidness, so on the spiritual plane he
represents the possibility of a personal redemption from
what appears to be a hopelessly perverse, sinful, and excessively rational life. "There it is, peaceful and pure
life," (II, 29) Login admits while viewing Tolya. The
surge of positive emotion which Login feels at this moment recalls a scene in *Crime and Punishment*, where a
child—Marmeladov's young step-daughter, Polenka—similarly affects the hero, who "finds a certain happiness in
looking at her."[13] The combination of the little girl's
naiveté and the kiss which she gives Raskolnikov produces
a warmth in his soul as it simultaneously reveals within
him a desire to move closer to life and to accept and
love it at any cost. Raskolnikov does not finish his remark to Razumikin, when he admits that "I have just been
kissed by a creature who, even if I killed anybody, would
still...,"[14] but the implication is clear that what
soothes him is the knowledge that Polenka's love and acceptance of him are guaranteed despite his sinful nature.
Sologub's protagonist is similarly moved by children.
His association with them also serves as a reminder of
his striving toward a higher state of spiritual perfection and as a demonstration of his possible worthiness of
attaining it.

Already in *Bad Dreams* the child is associated with
the crucial disparity between the real and the ideal and
he unfailingly represents the beauty of the latter. Tolya
and Lenya at all times embody a sense of apartness, a
preferable otherness. Yet, this is not a state which, as
in Sologub's later fiction, assumes a more purely symbolist distinction of two separate levels of reality, of
a suprarational realm of individualized dream (*The Petty
Demon*) or fantasy (*A Legend in Creation*). Rather, it is
one which bears full allegiance to the everyday world.
At this first stage of Sologub's career, his children
represent, and his hero wishes to achieve, a very earthly,
wholesomely pastoral and recognizably romantic ideal.
The direction of escape is a return to a kind of primi-

tive, Rousseauistic state of uncomplicated innocence and
natural purity. "They're still developing," Login says
of his pupils, "and we're beginning to fall apart.
They're taking from life everything they can to themselves and for themselves; we, weary under the burden of
our load, unburden ourselves, throw to the wind as much
as possible" (II, 197). Login further reveals the connection between the singular quality of the special
child's status and the specific nature of his own goal
when he asserts:

> The greater society's knowledge and intelli-
> gence the clearer it becomes that the sources
> of life are drying up. That is why, I think,
> people of our age are so cruel to children;
> we envy their naive simplicity (II, 227).

This lack of artificiality explains Login's interest
in "living life," a Dostoevskian-inspired notion which we
discussed more fully in conjunction with Sologub's nature
stories. Implicit here is the rejection of socially corrupt, man-made institutions—for example, the school
where Login teaches—which remove a person from his own
inherent goodness and from life's natural rhythms. An
equally important ingredient in Login's ideal of "living
life" is the criticism of reason as the primary force
which guides human behavior. Significantly, Sologub's
hero is referred to at one point as "Mr. Login—Hamlet,
Prince of Denmark." (II, 167) The brooding, overly critical, and self-searching nature of Login - Hamlet is
countered by the children in *Bad Dreams*, who, Login admits,
are close to "the sources of life" and unencumbered by
guilt and doubt.
      That Lenya in particular is close to life's sources
and nature's rhythms is evident from his peculiarly visionary role in the novel's plot. He intuits things
which go unnoticed by adults, and at times he must even
prod Login into recognizing Anna's love for him. He is
surely "father to the man" when, at the end of *Bad
Dreams*, he senses trouble for the hero and leads him to
safety. His part in reuniting Login with Anna, so that
she may cure the wounds inflicted on him by hostile local crowds, as well as his subsequent advice to leave
town, symbolically demonstrate the child's crucial role
in directing the hero to the transformation he is to undergo in his "new life." It is this "new life" which the

novel's conclusion promises but does not illustrate. Like
her counterpart Sonya Marmelodova in *Crime and Punishment*, although without any of her Christian overtones,
Anna represents the full, unquestioning acceptance of
life, and it is she who draws the transgressor-hero to
it.

When the novel closes, Anna exits with Login, as
Sonya departs with Raskolnikov, to an allegedly brighter,
more meaningful existence. But such a communion has not
been achieved without the assistance of the child. Tolya
and Lenya serve as vital intermediaries to what Anna
represents in the novel: the hope for spiritual transformation and moral rebirth. She is, as Login once calls
her, a "fairy tale"—the wish for a life which can be made
endlessly lovely and enchanting. But only by first recognizing that he was—and still can be—what the positive
children symbolize, is Login finally ready to join Anna
and submit to the idea which she embodies. Lenya's continual encouragement of Login's interest in Anna culminates in his literal uniting of the two at the end of
the novel. Significantly, once this is accomplished,
once he has convinced Login of his worthiness of achieving the ideal, he is left behind—as is Tolya. The
children are no longer needed in the transfiguration
which is about to occur.

* * * * *

In *Bad Dreams* the child symbolizes, and inspires the
hero to seek, a pristine state of natural purity which
negates the sordidness of surrounding life. Yet, if
Sologub's depiction of this character in his first novel
was fairly traditional, with its recognizably Rousseauistic overtones (which, for example, Lenya's initial appearance in the forest evokes), then his presentation of
the positive child in his second novel was assuredly different. Not that the pattern in *The Petty Demon*, or for
that matter *A Legend in Creation*, changes. The child's
central position in the positive hero's search for a
transcendent ideal remains symptomatically similar in
each and ultimately reveals, as we shall see, the special
status which novelistic plotting holds in the larger body
of Sologub's work. Nor does the difference in presentation reflect, recalling Bely, Sologub's weakening ties to
Russian reality in *The Petty Demon*. Both the sordid details which the writer uses to recreate the provincial

setting and his obvious interest in the effect of social
milieu on character are as evident here as they are in
its predecessor. Instead, any variation in the child's
depiction has largely to do with the fact that *The Petty
Demon* is more fully a decadent and symbolist novel than
Bad Dreams, and it is as different in its presentation of
material as it is in its vision of the world. The
chronological sequence of Sologub's novels never reveals
a decreasing concern with the vulgar, banal, and specious
aspects of life,—what is known as *poshlost*; it does,
however, exhibit the different and more urgent ways in
which the writer chooses to reject them. For what is
patently obvious here is not Sologub's growing disregard
for life's ugly truth, but instead his increasing belief
in its attractive uniqueness, to which his children bear
greatest witness. Thus, Sasha Pylnikov is legitimately
a part of the environment which Sologub depicts in *The
Petty Demon*, a part of the realism which the author never
fully abandoned. Yet at the same time he may be seen as
suggesting its unquestioned antithesis.

Readers did not need to wait for Modest Gofman's
conclusion in 1909 that "the distinguishing feature of
symbolism is its realism,"[15] in order to make the connection between the two in Sologub's novel. The realist
foundations of what has frequently been regarded as the
finest example of early twentieth-century Russian symbolist prose had already been acclaimed by Blok, when *The
Petty Demon* first appeared in a separate edition (1907).
The following year, Bely observed that "the realism of
our [generation's, S.R.] literature began with Čexov and
and is ending with Sologub."[16] What Bely means is that
Sologub, like Chekhov, continues to focus on Russian
provincial life and to uncover its unsavory aspects, much
as did the earlier proponents of this "realist" tradition, Gogol and Saltykov-Schedrin. Of course, the
decadent coloring of Sologub's prose—his morbid fascination with death and decay, his preoccupation with the
erotic and with various forms of sexual perversion—was
unmistakable to Bely, but this did not obscure for him
the more fundamental literary style which underlie both
the writer's depiction of milieu and his method of characterization.

To the extent that the child reveals the different
components of such a literary style, the study of this
figure is particularly useful. Sasha provides an excellent example of Sologub's ability to combine his most

sensually provocative subject matter with his most psy-
chologically-oriented detail. Psychological portraiture
is considered to be a major feature of realist fiction,
and in his depiction of Sasha Pylnikov, Sologub creates
one of his most emotionally dynamic characters. The
child does undergo evolution; and his innermost mental
processes are, if not always uncovered, then at least
suggested as he responds to a variety of different situations.

Peredonov's fall is not a very great one from his
initial defilement of his apartment and his cohabitant
to his ultimate murder of his best friend. Emotional
sensitivity is hardly possible in a "consciousness
(which) was a depraved and dead apparatus" (141). Nor
is there much attempt at penetrating Ludmila's psyche
(in contrast to Login's characterization) in order more
accurately to justify the motivation for her escapist
behavior or, as in Sasha's case, to trace the psychosexual ramifications of her involvement with her young
companion. But in the depiction of the process of
Sasha's adolescent maturation there is, as we have seen,
a true sense of development. Equally unique is the
warmth with which Sologub approaches this character. In
fact, such an intimate penetration of the child explains
what we may call his "demythicization," which careful
readers of Sologub might well have noticed in Sasha's
presentation.

"And your mother will punish you?" Peredonov asks,
as he contemplates accusing the boy of using foul language. "'I have no mother,' Sasha said, 'my mother died
long ago...'" (181). This is a stock situation, a code
phrase which is prevalent in Sologub's treatment of
children beginning in 1896 and which can be called the
theme of the white mother, after a story by the same
name ("Belaja mama," 1898). In that piece, later on
with the hero's son Kirsha in A Legend in Creation, and
in the stories "In Captivity," "Turandina" (1912), and
others, the melancholy and grief-stricken child pines
away for his real, "white" mother who lives in another
land, while he is abandoned on earth, imprisoned by an
evil sorceress—his "black" mother. Noticing this pattern as early as 1909, Chukovsky[17] realized its relation
to one of the basic myths which underlies Sologub's art;
namely, that beauty (the white mother) is far away and
unreachable, appearing only in dreams, visions, and
memory. Only the child, who bears the strongest traces

of this former existence, is painfully aware of its loss.
However, in his attempt to provide Sasha's characterization with psychological veracity, Sologub eliminates the
fairy-tale aspect of the white mother theme, although its
connotations invariably come to mind. As we have seen,
Sologub's treatment of "spring's awakening" in Sasha suggests the child's abandonment of the special, removed
state of "otherness" as he becomes increasingly attracted
to its antithesis. Unlike his counterparts in the stories, the boy is not a dreamy or visionary character, nor
does he exhibit a hostility toward his surroundings due
to any extraterrestrial loyalties. In fact, it is precisely his earthiness which Ludmila immediately notices
and which she seeks to remove. The observation that
"(Ludmila) had thought about taking the perfume with her
even before, in order to scent the student so that he
couldn't smell from his offensive Latin, ink, and boyish-
ness" (228), suggests, especially in the use of the
final word "mal'čičestvo" ("the quality of being a boy"),
a normality and typicality which characterize Sasha.

        Yet to skirt fantasy in order to preserve the inher-
ent realism of the child's portrayal is not to admit that
beyond the real there cannot be, or is not, an otherness
which transcends the literalness of a phenomenon and imparts to it additional significance. I. Mashbats-Verov
notes this when he claims that "numerous prose works of
... Sologub are built on this principle: behind external,
seemingly real events there is always depicted the in-
authenticity of real life and, on the contrary, the
'reality' of dream, game, 'shadows' (is depicted)..."[18]
In the case of *The Petty Demon* one would expect even the
most realistic image or event to betray a certain mysteriousness and inconsistency. The novel achieves its
unique effect precisely from the infectious transmission
of a neurotic tone and unstable world-view which reflects
the conviction that all things may be other than what
they seem. That "neutral" words themselves can imply
something which they do not immediately signify is attested to largely by the use of puns in the novel. In
one of the many examples of linguistic instability,
Sasha notices Ludmila's power to make two unrelated words
merge together and thus suggest a similar meaning merely
by their acoustical likeness. "You're a funny one!" he
tells her, "glycerine (glicerinovoe) and green grapes
(vinograd)—they're completely different words, but you
make them sound the same" (207). The capacity of lan-

guage itself to transform the "real" or the actual into a
completely different order is a theme which we shall consider later. Here we need only note that various phenomena in *The Petty Demon* contain hidden dimensions which
transcend objectively "fixed" borders and lead in other
directions. In this regard, Bely's comparison of Sologub
to Gogol is worth recalling: "from the depths of symbolism Gogol etched the formula of realism: he is its alpha;
from the depths of realism Sologub etched the formula of
the fantastic—the *nedotykomka*, elkič, etc.: he is the
omega of realism."[19] Bely's sequence "from realism to
symbolism" suggests a shift in Sologub's writing or at
least a combination of somewhat disparate, even contradictory elements. From his fundamental roots of "provincial realism," which was mentioned above in regard to
another of Bely's statements about the writer, Sologub
develops into an artist who increasingly employs anti-
or non-realist devices, such as Bely itemizes. While
Sasha does not exemplify the presence of the fantastic
beneath the real or the movement of the natural to the
supernatural (a function which children will perform in
A Legend in Creation), he does reflect the unknown behind the visible, the shift from clarity to mystery.

By their second meeting, Ludmila calls Sasha her
"young, mysterious person" (236), already sensing in him
a hidden potential to which she is immediately attracted.
In place of the badges of Sasha's everyday existence—the
books, the ink, the academic concerns—Ludmila wants to
create a higher, more ethereal world of beauty. Much of
her activity with Sasha represents an idealization of the
child, an envisioning of him as someone who stands above
the ordinary, humdrum quality of life which everywhere
surrounds them. Such is the case in her symbolic dream
of the boy as a white swan, in which she imagines a situation where "it smelled of slime and stale water and of
grass decaying because of the sultriness, but along the
water, dark and evilly peaceful, floated a white swan,
strong and majestically sovereign" (212). The contrast
here is between the real and the ideal, between the vileness of life the way it is, *Peredonovism*, and the magic
of life the way it should be: beautiful and enchanting.
As Ludmila's relationship with Sasha demonstrates, if she
cannot find ecstasy and joy in the norm of everyday
reality, then she will transform this realm and provide
these qualities herself. "I love beauty...," Ludmila
tells Sasha, revealing her pagan-like sensuality. "I

love the body, strong, agile, naked, and capable of enjoyment" (356). Through her symbolic redressing of this
body and her continual "reshaping" of this figure to embody a different image of loveliness, the child passes
from merely an exceptional type of schoolboy (but a
schoolboy nevertheless) to the exalted cult figure of a
boy-god.

   "The human body," Ivanov-Razumnik reminds us, "is
for Sologub the embodiment of beauty,"[20] and Ludmila's
worship of Sasha's naked flesh exemplifies an idealism
which is openly amoral in its striving for perfection.
Ludmila's search for beauty is stripped of the Rousseau-
ist connotations and natural, earthly allegiances it had
for Login in *Bad Dreams*. In that novel, the child could
lead the hero to his "new life," but himself was not a
part of it. In *The Petty Demon*, the situation is quite
different. Here the child's body as such symbolizes
Ludmila's perfect ideal. Beauty is seen to exist *above*
nature, emancipated from earthly values such as good and
evil and existing as an absolute in itself. Ludmila's
inspiration bears the stamp not so much of the terres-
trial realm, but rather of a separate world of mystery
and spirit which her individual will alone creates. The
very amorality and "unnaturalness" of this beauty signifies the desired release from all earthly bonds into a
world governed solely by laws of the all-powerful "I".

   Decadent and amoral overtones which are associated
with Ludmila's spiritualization of Sasha should not,
however, be overplayed, as Ivanov-Razumnik stresses, if
we are to appreciate the more important connotations
which the couple's relationship infers. However ethical-
ly indifferent Ludmila may be in her adoration of Sasha,
she nonetheless views the child's body not as an object
for defilement—as Grushina's and Vershina's previously
beautiful bodies have been, but rather as a subject for
her escapist dream by which she seeks refuge from dehu-
manizing life. Sasha's existence serves as additional
proof of life's evil for Peredonov, dragging him down
into the mire of paranoiac fear and vulgarity. For
Ludmila, however, this same reality becomes a symbol for
nature's exciting potential, raising her to the heights
of rhapsody and creative fantasy. To relate this contrast in terms of the dream about the swan, Peredonov
prefers to see Sasha as part of the stale and sultry
realm of material reality, whereas Ludmila insists on
negating realism, as it were, by viewing this same person

in terms of the divine. "The deed of the lyric poet ...
is ... by the force of charm and daring to direct the in-
ertly earthly to the embodiment of beautiful form,"[21]
Sologub would write some years later. No clearer defense
of Ludmila's activity of transforming the ordinary into
the sacred, and of converting "realism" into a "higher
realism," could exist. Ludmila's activity with Sasha
continually reflects a dissatisfaction with the *status
quo* of what he, and more broadly, life is. Her activity
betrays a desire to mold life into the more appealing
substance which its hidden potential suggests it is capable of becoming.

Sasha's role in Ludmila's dream certainly makes obvious her craving for a transcendent ideal. Yet, the
questionability of whether she achieves it does not imply
the inherent impossibility of imposing a mystical vision
upon an essentially material world. Instead, it can be
argued that the major impediment in Ludmila's desired
escape from the confines of banal reality is, at least
as Vyacheslav Ivanov saw it, a lack of faith. In a review of an earlier collection of Sologub's stories,
Ivanov laments the absence of an affirmative substitute
to fill the void which the writer's rejection of the
here-and-now engenders. The terms here are fully applicable to the situation in *The Petty Demon.*

> In this book of mystery there is no excitement
> of faith and no hope for transformation. It
> tempts the spirit to a final "no," but this
> spirit, which is obstinate, does not completely
> renounce its primordial claims to a life lived
> in terms of the sweet aspects of a joyous
> "yes."[22]

Applying Ivanov's observation to Sologub's novel,
one would underline Ludmila's inability to renounce completely the desires and passions which characterize the
very material existence which she seeks to transcend.
So accustomed is she to the habit and routine of ordinary life (Ivanov's "sweet aspects of the joyous 'yes'"),
that Ludmila cannot extend her sense of mystery beyond
what proves to be a markedly earthly fascination with
Sasha's flesh. For Sologub sexual passion is a sign of
man's base instincts and is, by definition, a barrier to
total bliss. The ideal in his fiction, particularly between the male/female protagonists of *Bad Dreams* (Login

and Anna) and *A Legend in Creation* (Trirodov and Elisaveta) is "love without desire." But Ludmila's realm of
pure spirit seems insufficiently powerful to eradicate
fully traces of material desire. Thus, Ivanov's argument
would run, in *The Petty Demon* the power of Sologub's
darkness ultimately overshadows any rays of light which
may occasionally penetrate into it, for it is a stronger
force which draws the writer earthward than to the beyond. What calls into question the success of Ludmila's
transformation is the lack of commitment to a thoroughly
antithetical alternative to the realm of the everyday,
the absence of a conviction which would completely re-
pudiate the world of the "yes" by definitively proclaim-
ing an unequivocal "no." Such equivocation is reflected
in, and really predictable from, the very portrayal of
the embodiment of the ideal itself, Sasha Pylnikov.

As always, Sologub's literary style reflects key
elements of his philosophy. Where the writer's pr.sen-
tation of material is exceptional and hyperbolic, yet
rationally feasible nevertheless; where the "otherness"
which Sasha represents is mysterious but still plausible,
the margin for belief in the suprareal transcendental
order, in whose light everyday reality would be wholly
transformed, is narrow. But when Sologub's "realism"
moves more fully toward the fantastic, as Bely noted,
the "excitement of faith," which Ivanov finds lacking in
him, is manifested. Only when his style begins to transcend the limits of the empirical, would the possibility
of reaching the ideal be firmly secure. This happens in
A Legend in Creation, and it is reflected precisely in
the utterly unique depiction of Kirsha and the supernatural "quiet children."

* * * * *

In *The Petty Demon* Sologub was clearly skeptical
about man's ability to realize his positive ideal of redemptive beauty within the borders of empirical, everyday existence. But by the time he had embarked upon *A
Legend in Creation*, he believed that this goal could be
achieved through an individual's own resources in the
world of the imagination. The trilogy itself—*Drops of
Blood (Kapli krovi*, 1907); *Queen Ortruda (Koroleva
Ortruda*, 1909); *Smoke and Ashes (Dym i pepel*, 1913)—the
first and last parts of which will presently concern us,
is Sologub's most imaginative work. It is in its own way

a triumph of creative inventiveness, where elements of
the most original fantasy comingle with the ordinary
events of everyday existence. "An intricate weaving of
the most abstract fantasy and the crudist reality, of romantic fictions and daily contemporaneity, of a scientific utopia and a metaphysical dream,"[23] Gornfeld had
characterized the work, although not without complaining,
perhaps too strongly, of its aesthetic weakness.   Scenes
which depict the social ferment and political turmoil indigenous to the period of Russia's 1905 revolution al-
ternate with descriptions of the bizarre adventures of
the protagonist, the chemist, inventor, and literateur,
Trirodov. Like his predecessors Login and Ludmila, he
strives continually to escape his current boredom. Gornfeld's charge of structural incoherence is valid only if
one insists upon viewing the shifts between the real and
the fantastic as arbitrary, instead of recognizing the
fundamental way in which one serves the other. What is
distinctive here (and this is something which might create in a reader the erroneous impression of Sologub's
ultimate irreconcilability with life) is the greater
difference, the wider gap which exists between the traditional Sologubian antitheses. The "here" is the writer's
most sociopolitical account, his most detailed representation of current events; the "there" is Sologub's furthest removed and least empirically valid realm.   It is
a paradox, but ultimately not a surprising one, that
Sologub's most contemporary work strives hardest to destroy the illusion of its own realism.

     Nor is it insignificant that the novel which is most
deeply grounded in the historical present looks furthest
ahead toward the utopian future. The broader the basis
of Sologub's criticism of contemporary life, the larger
seems to be the scale of his reaction against it.
Trirodov's desired release from reality does not cul-
minate in merely a private bedroom dream, as in Ludmila's
case; instead, it embodies an entire world, a complete
blueprint for an alternative system. "We live here all
day; we eat, study and play—all here.... We are fleeing
the beast, fleeing the wilderness of the cities" (XVIII,
13), reports one of the teachers of the colony which
Trirodov has established on his estate. Trirodov's plan
to transport this perfect society onto the United
Islands, his magical voyage to the beautiful planet of
Oile, "where a century had passed, yet on earth only a
second elapsed" (XX, 47), his desire to visit the moon—

all contribute to the book's futuristic quality and its
mytho-poetic orientation toward dream and fairy-tale.
Such an orientation makes *A Legend in Creation* the purest
example of Sologub's symbolism, particularly if one
agrees with the claim of one of the movement's prominent
theoreticians, Ellis,* that "despite sharp internal differences, a common trait unites all the symbolists: all
of their branchings, all of their newer and newer subtle-
ties are directed toward the future...."[24]

Not only are the opposites in *A Legend in Creation*
more extreme, they are more evenly weighted. The preoccupation with escape, which represented a relatively in-
substantial airhole in *Bad Dreams* or a brief interlude
in *The Petty Demon*, achieves coequal status in Sologub's
trilogy. Consequently, with reference to *A Legend in
Creation* it is impossible even to consider "(Sologub's)
sharp turn off the main-travelled roads of naturalism"[25]
as "an episode ... which is almost unconnected to the
(major plot) line ... a circumstantial story,"[26] as
Gornfeld had done regarding the Sasha-Ludmila scenes of
The Petty Demon. The antidote to *poshlost*—what Blok
had labeled the "window into springtime"—is no longer
in a subordinate position, either thematically or struc-
turally. Nor is it consciously set off or noticeably
removed from what in the other novels constitutes the
main story line. Many scenes reveal the complete and
extremely matter-of-fact assimilation of the novel's
fantastic elements into the realm of the real. These
include the presence of Trirodov's deceased wife at a
masquerade party, where she chats with the other guests
(both the live and the dead ones), Trirodov's conversation with Christ, who comes disguised as Prince Emanuil
Osipovich Davydov, and the quiet children's miraculous
rescue of the heroine, Elisaveta, from the hands of some
lustful drunkards by hypnotizing her captors. Unlike *The
Petty Demon*, where the fantastic *nedotykomka* could be
explained as purely an hallucination of Peredonov's deranged mind, the supernatural elements in *A Legend in
Creation* are not the product of insanity.

Here mysterious phenomena appear as normal events
of the real world, with which they naturally coexist.
This "democratic" integration of levels reflects one of
the work's fundamental philosophical principles, which
Kirsha and the quiet children will come best to symbol-

*Pseudonym for L. L. Kobylinsky.

ize; namely, that dream, fantasy, visions of beauty can
and must be an inseparable part of our ordinary everyday
existence. Anna Ermolina says as much when she assures
Login near the conclusion of *Bad Dreams* that: "we shall
love each other and, like gods, we shall create and we
shall build a new heaven and a new earth" (II, 337). In
fact, the struggle between the fantastic and the ordinary
and the ability of the former to participate actively,
and ultimately to triumph in the latter, constitutes the
central focus of the trilogy, as the author admits.

> Ordinary life is evil and irritating; it
> trudges along and endeavors to defame (our)
> sweet inventions and to spatter with the
> abominable filth of its noisy streets your
> beautiful, gentle, pensive face, Dream!
> Who will eventually win? Every-day reality,
> polluted by all of the rotten poisons of the
> past ... or you, dear (Dream) ... dropping
> one after the other, your light, semi-
> transparent, and multi-colored veil in order
> to present in solemn illumination your eter-
> nal beauty? (XIX, 3)

The basic tension in the trilogy results from the
clash between the reality of the world in its objective
and ugly authenticity and the reality of man's personal
vision of it as a potentially beautiful ideal. "One life
is not enough for me—I want to create many others"
(XX, 55-56), Trirodov confesses, implying that the everyday constitutes only one form of existence, to which he
refuses to be bound. This remark recalls Login's query,
"Why the niggardly fate of having only one life?" (II,
117), but unlike his forerunner, Trirodov proceeds to
correct this problem. *A Legend in Creation* represents
Sologub's culminating work. In it, and primarily through
the words and deeds of his protagonist, Sologub makes his
final response to issues which have concerned him in his
previous two novels, as well as in most of his prose,
poetry, and drama.

That *A Legend in Creation* constitutes Sologub's most
ambitious attempt at presenting other worlds, at offering
different alternatives to "reality" via the most extreme
form of fantastic realism is hardly surprising when one
considers the uniqueness of its protagonist. Trirodov is
a poet, a maker of fictions: Sologub's only artist-hero.

Indeed, in its essence, *A Legend in Creation* is a work
devoted to the problems of art and to the nature of the
creative process as such, to which the book's unreal, unbelievable, and extraordinary elements strongly attest.
Trirodov's statement that "the very life which we are
creating here represents a combination of elements of
real life with fantastic and utopian elements" (XVIII,
101) is as much a description of the book in which such
action transpires as it is an explanation of his own
activities. The trilogy itself is its own testament to
the underlying aesthetic and philosophical assumption
which is at work in it: the autonomy of the creative will
and the power of the human imagination to soar above life
and ultimately to shape it. "I take a piece of life,
crude and poor, and I create from it a legend—for I am a
poet" (XVIII, 3) reads the opening of the trilogy. What
Sologub confesses to be his purpose as a novelist is
nothing less than the goal of his fictional hero. The
very existence of *A Legend in Creation* as a genuine entity symbolizes what the story of Trirodov is largely
about: the possibility, through creative fantasy, of
concretizing man's most imaginative visions and highest
ideals. Referring to *A Legend in Creation*, Dolinin observes that "Sologub creates his legends of unearthly
dreams and visions, his mysterious world (which is) so
unlike our usual world."[27] The writer's conception of
otherness here—as his children clearly attest—is undoubtedly his most magical and irreal. Yet Dolinin's
evaluation fails to consider that the fantastic itself
can contain within it a certain reality, and thus the art
which faithfully depicts it can also be a form of realism. "I have my own view of reality (in art) and what
most people call almost fantastic and exceptional is for
me sometimes the very essence of the real,"[28] Dostoevsky had written, defending his use of the extraordinary
and exceptional in art as a unique brand of realism. In
Sologub the fantastic, particularly as it is used in the
depiction of children, is not capricious or arbitrary,
nor does it represent merely a curious and ingeniously
diversionary entertainment. It has a higher, serious
purpose and a poetic truth of its own. "Does the fantastic have the right to exist in art?" Dostoevsky asked
in a letter to Turgenev. "Well who cares to answer such
questions! If there is anything that might be criticized in *The Phanthoms* it is this: It is not quite fantastic enough."[29] For Sologub, as well as for Dostoev-

sky, what is genuine is man's quest for a higher truth,
even if it is sought beyond the earthly in the realm of
the fantastic. And whereas Sologub's most extraordinary
creations, Kirsha and the quiet children, demonstrate the
fantasy which is often resorted to in the quest for perfection, they nevertheless indicate what is for their
creator the most essential reality of all: the search for
the ideal itself. It is no accident that of all fiction,
Cervantes' novel *Don Quixote* had the greatest influence
on Sologub. The novel's theme of man's quest to find
lofty, even if at times impracticable, ideals in life
attracted Sologub during his entire career. The cerebral, introspective Hamlet-like hero of Sologub's first
novel is replaced by, transformed into, the Quixote-like
dreamer-fantast of his last novel of the decadent-symbolist period.

Two basic themes dominate Trirodov's story: man's
reconciliation with a former beauty which he has once
known and his transformation of his present existence
into a new loveliness which he wants to establish. Once
the first has taken place, the second is ready to materi-
alize. Kirsha is tied to the first theme, the mystical
legend of the past; the quiet children are associated
with the second theme, the utopian vision of the future.

In the characterization of Trirodov's son Kirsha,
Sologub displays—to use Zamyatin's apt description of
the trilogy as a whole—"the fine and difficult art of
bringing together within a single formula both the solid
and gaseous states of literary matter, the everyday and
the fantastic."[30] Unlike the quiet children, Kirsha's
movements are not restricted solely to Trirodov's walled-
in estate. He passes freely, and symbolically, from the
outside world, where he has contacts with the town's inhabitants, to the enchanted forest where his father's
adolescent colony is installed. Although psychologically, Kirsha's portrayal is far less complex than Sasha
Pylnikov's, Sologub does attempt—if only briefly—to
convey the child's emotional anguish which is caused by
the torments of earthly life. It is specifically when
longing for his deceased mother that Kirsha displays the
pitiful sadness so typical of his predecessors in the
stories.

> Kirsha impatiently ... wanted his mother to
> come. Why did Kirsha want this? He himself
> did not know. Thus, the poor child's heart

pined away, stung by strange and secret desires (XX, 35).

This is, once again, a reworking of the "white mother"
theme, here enveloped in the kind of mystery which Sologub so studiously avoided in *The Petty Demon*. An external force, over which the child has no control, draws
him to another world, the knowledge of which has still
not been eradicated from his consciousness. Whether he
is standing before a window "seemingly looking into the
far-off ... as people do when they are hallucinating"
(XVIII, 294), or whether he is stirred by "dark fore-
bodings," as he is when he predicts the rising of the
dead, the clairvoyant Kirsha is pervaded by an eeriness,
thoroughly unknown to Sologub's previous children. The
presentation of the child as a character who blends so
harmoniously into the novel's atmosphere of magic, sor-
cery, and witchcraft demonstrates Sologub's ability to
create the most varied and original child types throughout the many years of his literary career. There are
for each of his moods and for every phase of his literary career appropriate children to reflect his current
emotional and ideological state.

Just as in terms of characterization Kirsha is a
kind of alloy, embodying, and alternating between, the
real and the fantastic, so in regard to the plot he is
an intermediary figure, serving as mediator between two
worlds. The son of the first "mysterious" wife of
Trirodov (who erroneously, though meaningfully, associates him with her death—as if to emphasize his succes-
sion to the tradition which she represents), Kirsha
serves as a reinforcement of what the hero was and again
hopes to be. This theme of the resurrection of, and
reconciliation to, a past perfection is a recurrent one
in the work, as it is directly sounded in the haunting
whispers of the moon, "What was will be again / What was
will be for more than once" ("Čto bylo, budet vnov' /
Čto bylo, budet ne odnaždy," XVIII, 115).[31] The child
is, in fact, an externalization of Trirodov's memory of
this past ideal state from which he is now detached; he
establishes the hero's original tie to absolute beauty
and suggests the validity of his desire to recapture it.
Lenya, we should recall, performs a similar function in
Bad Dreams. But as if to underscore the greater authenticity of man's claim to this once-known perfection,
Sologub makes its symbol the hero's *natural* son, as

opposed to his adopted child, as is the case in the
Login-Lenya relationship. If man's belief in the existence of lost paradise seems fantastic, then the presence
of Kirsha proves the contrary.

Trirodov's remembrance of a former existence is
tied to a myth which in 1907 had found a prominent place
in Sologub's poetry and which underlies the story line in
A Legend in Creation. Originally man before the Fall
lived in innocence and harmony with his first wife, "the
moon-like dream Lilit, pervaded by quiet and secrecy"
(XX, 34-35), who subsequently, after his expulsion from
paradise, has come to symbolize his lost ideal. Man
currently exists in the era of his second wife, "the
sunny, deep-blue, golden Eve-Elisaveta" (XX, 34), to
whom he hesitates being reconciled because of her embodiment of all that is ordinary and real. Kirsha is
central to the plot, for it is he who reconciles these
two opposing states by urging the hero to accept the
latter without sacrificing the former. "I feel that you
must let (Elizaveta and Elena) in. They are interesting
girls.... The older one somehow resembles mother"
(XVIII, 20), Kirsha says of the heroine and her younger
sister, advising the reluctant father to permit them entry into his estate. As the living reminder of
Trirodov's beautiful past, *in illo tempore*, Kirsha has
the greatest right and the strongest authority to shape
his future. This he does by initiating a process that
culminates in Trirodov's "loving Elisaveta—(which)
means loving and accepting the world, the whole world"
(XVIII, 159).

However, accepting the reality of the present and
reconciling it with the ideal of the past represents
only part of the process of man's establishment of order
and meaning in his life. Trirodov already initiated
this process of reconciliation with *temps perdu* by symbolically transposing his utopian past into his current
existence through the establishment of the adolescent
paradise on his estate. Close to nature and removed
from life's evil and sinfulness, Sologub's latter-day
Garden recalls, both in the language and tone of its
description, the serenely beautiful land of the hero's
miraculous vision in Dostoevsky's "Dream of a Ridiculous
Man." In Dostoevsky's story, fantasy also assumes a
reality all of its own, determining the behavior of the
protagonist who, like Trirodov, devotes his life to
preaching the truth of his dreams and to striving for

their earthly realization. Trirodov's colony perfectly
realizes, as does the vision of Dostoevsky's dreamer,
Login's and Ludmila's ideal of nakedness without shame,
of pure, unadorned beauty free from sensual desires and
possessive impulses.

Yet Trirodov's youthful colony does not stand alone.
Alongside it exists the strange group of quiet children,
which suggests that the attempt to restore the ideal past
is only one component in the hero's search for happiness.
Referring to his adolescent colony, Trirodov does con-
fess that "I shall once again become simple and gentle
... like my dear children" (XVIII, 242-243). This remark
undoubtedly prompted Andrew Field to conclude—with only
partial correctness—that "the prophetic vision of *The
Created Legend*, quite simply put, is a return to innocence."[32]   But if the vision were so simple or its finality so absolute, then Trirodov's pastoral utopia, intro-
duced at the very beginning of *Drops of Blood*, would not
only suffice to represent his goal but would also, by
definition, symbolize the end of his strivings. That
this is not the case is borne out by the remainder of
the work as well as by its title. Field's translation,
The Created Legend, imparts a finality which is as misleading as is his assessment of Trirodov's goal. As the
present active participle, "tvorimaja"—"in creation" or
"being created"—implies, the emphasis here is less on
what the legend or goal actually is, than on the specific
process of its achievement.[33]   And it is this notion of
process which distinguishes *A Legend in Creation* as the
most unambiguous reflection of Sologub's mature thought.
Not reconciliation with the past via a recapturing of
its essence, which Sologub had already offered somewhat
vaguely in *Bad Dreams*, but transformation—not occasional, but continual transformation—is the crucial factor
in man's search for his cherished ideal. It is this
idea which Sologub's most fantastic and most original
literary creations, the quiet children, symbolize; namely, that in order to reach the ideal man needs constantly to create it. The notion of creation, of actively
transforming the present into something other than what
it is, rather than the return to, or restoration of,
some former blissful state, more faithfully represents
the work's prophetic vision. Johannes Holthusen corroborates such a conclusion when he argues that "the
transformation and metamorphosis of life via the creation of a new artistic and ingenious reality is the most

central theme of the trilogy."[34]   Elisaveta directly conveys this idea when, substituting Cervantes' equivalents
of Dulcinea for Lilit (dream) and Aldonsa for Eve (reality), she reminds Trirodov that "Dulcinea is to be loved,
*but the fullness of life belongs to Aldonsa in the pro-
cess of becoming Dulcinea*" (XVIII, 234, my emphasis).
    The quiet children are vitally connected to what
Elisaveta calls "the process of becoming." If Kirsha
represents the need to realize the perfection of the past
and to incorporate it into the present, then these even
more miraculous characters, "next to whom (Kirsha) seemed
earthly ..." (XVIII, 238), symbolize the possibility of
using the present to create the beautiful future. En-
shrouded in a peaceful, grave-like aura, Sologub's quiet
children live totally apart from everyone else in
Trirodov's colony, having virtually no contact with the
outside world. "Their eyes don't look, but they see all;
their ears don't listen but they hear all" (XX, 168),
Trirodov claims, in a mysterious language which is appropriate to the children's own enigmatic nature. Their
cryptic silence has blatantly philosophical overtones,
for it signals the ultimate "no" to everyday reality.
These pale and strangely lifeless creatures are the absolute negation of all corruptive material desire and
earthly passion; they symbolize the rejection of the
routine and mundane in life for a higher, more exalted
and mysterious existence. "They want nothing" (XVIII,
114), Trirodov notes, emphasizing their nonparticipation
in any human activity. The sole preoccupation of these
creatures is their eerie nighttime ritual of swinging
gently in the garden and faintly singing as the moon
watches, enveloping them in its light. This practice,
incidentally, is not unknown to the inhabitants of
Dostoevsky's paradise in "The Dream of a Ridiculous
Man." They, too, "in the evening, before going to
sleep, loved to gather together and sing in melodious
and harmonious choirs."[35] Yet the child-singers in *A
Legend in Creation* have distinctly Sologubian features.
Their swinging suggests suspension in both time and
space; they move, but go nowhere; they are neither
wholly alive nor dead. Rather, they exist in some intermediate, neutral, timeless state which Holthusen
formulates as a "shadow existence." "Trirodov's children, however, are in reality not angels, they are not
cupids," the critic argues, "but resurrected death; they
are creatures who had died early and who now lead a new

shadow existence."[36]   In one sense, these characters are
a perfect blend and a final resolution of light ("svet")
and shadows ("teni"), the antagonism between which had
plagued Sologub from the earliest years of his literary
career.

Resurrected from the dead and possessing secret
powers which are used to predict the future and even to
propel Trirodov's space ship,[37] the quiet children are
the purest creations of Sologub's fantasy. However, a
failure to understand the higher truth which underlies
this fantasy, as well as the precise significance of the
post-mortem existence of the children who embody it, is
likely to lead to a misrepresentation of the work. Kor-
ney Chukovsky, for example, stresses exclusively the
death-like quality of the quiet children. But in doing
so, he undermines the connection of these characters to
the central theme of creative fantasy and thus inaccur-
ately concludes that *A Legend in Creation* is a "de-
frocking of (Sologub's) dream"[38] rather than its major
promulgation. The process by which the eleven year-old
Egorka becomes a quiet child sufficiently demonstrates
the victory of dream in *A Legend in Creation,* (Sologub
had written a play on this theme, *Dream the Conqueror,
Mečta Pobeditel'nica,* in 1912), and as such disproves
Chukovsky's contention that "only in the grave can any
Aldonsa become Dulcinea."[39]   Trirodov's involvement in
Egorka's transformation is the most striking dramatiza-
tion of the book's oft-quoted opening lines, for it un-
derlines the accessibility of beauty in man's life and
the role which artistic imagination, and not death,
plays in acquiring it. In his short prose fiction,
Sologub, chiefly through his children, had indeed argued
the advantages of substituting death for earthly reality. But *A Legend in Creation* represents a more positive and optimistic phase of the writer's career. Here
the child, specifically the quiet children, reveals
Sologub's belief not in death, but rather in the creative process, in art itself as a refuge from *poshlost*
and ordinariness.

It is significant that Egorka, like all the other
quiet children, comes from the poorest of backgrounds.
He is "from the earth" (XVIII, 236)—fully a product of
the town's lowest, more "naturalistic" elements—who
nevertheless is "an angel in a brown mask, covered with
stains of dirt and dust" (XVIII, 222). Trirodov's power
to resurrect the child and to make him a member of his

extraordinary colony shows both his ability to extract
beauty from the crudest matter as well as his belief,
which Sologub's symbolist art increasingly reflects, that
the miraculous never lies very far beneath the real.

Readers of *The Brothers Karamazov* will recall that
upon His appearance in Seville, Christ also proves his
miraculous, God-like powers by resurrecting a dead child.
The parallel here is evidently intentional: Trirodov is a
modern Christ who overcomes death by creating art—beautiful, perfect, and eternal.

"Come to me...," Trirodov commands the dormant
Egorka. "You are from the earth—and I shall not separate you from the earth. You are from me, you are mine,
you are me, come to me. Awaken" (XVIII, 236), the hero
continues, as he initiates the boy into his newly-ac-
quired special status. We can consider this moment a
response to, and fulfillment of, one of Login's desires,
when he ponders, "What bliss it would be if, at will, I
could abandon this hateful shell and move into the body
of that ragged and grubby little boy..." (II, 117).
Trirodov does not, of course, literally become a child
upon resurrecting Egorka. But figuratively, if the
hero's act is properly understood, he does achieve what
the childhood status has come to mean to him. Perhaps
more than any other single child, Egorka indicates the
Sologubian hero's commitment to transforming his ordinary
life into fairy-tale. "All that is beautiful in life has
become real through dream" (XX, 16), Trirodov declares,
and the metamorphosis of Egorka exemplifies the belief
that only the individual will of the creative artist can
make the everyday extraordinary. Beauty exists only when
we will it ourselves. Egorka's beauty becomes a reality
when Trirodov removes it from ordinary life to the higher
realm of the ideal, when he transports it to the fantastic level of personal dream. And through this same dream
Trirodov hopes to reshape the future and to reform the
entire United Islands, over which he will become, significantly, King. "Without faith in miracle it is impossible to live," Sologub had written in 1915. "The
miracle of transformation is impossible but it is necessary, (and) the resolution of this contradiction is
given to man only in the ecstasy of creation."[40]

Trirodov's act of transforming Egorka into a quiet
child represents nothing less than an example of the
creative process itself; it is on one level a description
of how art is produced. Indeed, one of Trirodov's

revelations, particularly in this sequence, is that art
arises from the very stuff of life, but in the process of
creation changes and transcends it. It is in this sense
that Sologub understands death in *A Legend in Creation*:
not only literally, as the morbid and absolute end of
earthly existence, but figuratively, as the necessary
termination of one state in the joyous process of creating another, more perfect one.

On several occasions the quiet children are regarded
as created objects, with the implication that they possess their own higher reality. At one point they are
compared to a "series of enchantingly beautiful poses,
drawn by someone on a dark curtain" (XVIII, 37), and
later Trirodov himself states that they are "perfect,
like creations of high art" (XX, 169). And when the hero
reveals to Elisaveta his secret, "which has led the quiet
children from the darkness of non-being to the quiet of
another existence" (XX, 38), he could be talking as much
about the transformation of "lifeless" matter into a
work of art as the revival of children from the dead. It
is only during the creative process that inert, common-
place matter, the "piece of life" mentioned in the work's
opening line, becomes miraculous beauty. What the entire quiet-children episode suggests is that although
the complete and permanent eradication of earthly evil
may be unrealizable, man's continual striving to create
its antidote is certainly an encouraging substitute. The
very number of quiet children and the frequency with
which the hero engages in their creation reflect
Trirodov's belief that man can neither completely enjoy
nor capture beauty in its fixity, forever freezing it in
permanent stasis. Rather, beauty is process, it is constant re-creation and regeneration; hence, the title of
the trilogy. Trirodov says as much when he declares,
"if one dream deceives (me), then I shall strive toward
another" (XX, 55). Along these lines, Holthusen justly
connects the role of the child to the novel's major
theme of creative fantasy as well as to the hero's attempts at self-transcendence which occur precisely via
this method.

> Artistic creation is for Trirodov a way back
> to the state of childhood and herein is the
> reason why his entire colony of children
> exists.[41]

We need only recall Login's remarks about degenerate adults as opposed to developing children, and Ludmila's stated preference for pre-pubescent boys who are on the verge of, but who have not reached maturity, to understand that Sologub's appreciation of the child is based largely on the latter's capacity for growth, fluctuation, and change. Their potential is synonymous with the potential of creativity itself.

Behind the hero's peculiar relationship to the quiet children is the Sologubian notion that creation is an act of faith, a life-affirming deed via which man's ideal can be realized and his self-purification be assured. What Ivanov had found lacking in the writer's early works, when he had observed in them no "excitement of belief and no hope for transformation," is present in full force in *A Legend in Creation*. That Sologub's most fantastically conceived and imaginatively executed characters should represent his most ardent belief in the possibility of miracle is entirely logical. The quiet children demonstrate the genuineness of Sologub's symbolism, for they reflect a vision of another sphere of human reality which is the writer's most ecstatic and idealistic. One might note here Helen Muchnic's interesting distinction between decadence and symbolism, since it helps to clarify the children's connection to a more positive and redemptive note which is sounded in Sologub's trilogy. "The decadents had nightmares and so yearned to get away from life," she writes, "while the symbolists had visions and sought to bring heaven and earth togehter."[42]   In *The Petty Demon*, where the decadent strain is fairly prominent (especially in Sologub's use of the child), a sustained, unambiguous positive vision is generally lacking; this vision's presence in Sologub's fantastic trilogy (again with particular regard to his use of children) distinguishes the piece as Sologub's most optimistic work.

The secureness of Sologub's faith in his longed-for transcendental otherness is best conveyed in the opening lines of a poem which was written in the same year as the trilogy's concluding volume (1913).

Ja verju, verju, verju, verju,
V sebja, v tebja, v moju zvezdu.
Ot žizni ničego ne ždu,
No vse že verju, verju, verju,
Vse v žizni veroju izmerju....

I believe, believe, believe, believe,
In myself, in you, in my star.
I expect nothing from life,
But still, I believe, believe, believe,
That I'll change everything in life with my faith.
(1913)

By the publication of *A Legend in Creation* a note of unquestionable optimism pervades Sologub's writing. Along
with such collections of stories as *The Book of Charms*
(Kniga očarovanij, 1909) and *The Book of Transformations*
(Kniga prevraščenij, 1913), the trilogy reveals the fulfillment of a philosophical attitude, articulated as
early as 1894: "Live and believe in deceptions, / Fairy
tales and dreams" ("Živi i ver' obmanam / I skazkam i
mečtam"). The desire to believe in the possibility of
building a new, higher reality exists from the earliest
years of Sologub's literary career. But only in the
later period could he write with such conviction that his
symbolist art "wants to create a new beauty, turbulently
and daringly, *from any material*, to attract any human
experience to that current via which the soul strives
for the high and the beautiful."[43] Sologub's formulation is, of course, dramatized in Trirodov's encounter
with Egorka, but what its ultimate significance reflects
is a final reconciliation in his writing between the
disparate elements of the "here" and the "there."
　　　Just as, stylistically, realism had always been the
starting point of Sologub's symbolism, so philosophically, the empirical and everyday fulfills a similar function, serving to fuel the ideal itself. In the Egorka
episode the boy's "black mother," who epitomizes crude,
ordinary life, kills the child, failing to appreciate
the beauty within him. The dreamer-visionary Trirodov,
however, perceives this hidden potential and, rather
than disregard it, he commits himself to making it, via
the magic of his imagination, a vital factor of his
existence. Trirodov's use of the quiet children's special energy to launch his rocket ship also contains obvious symbolic connotations. Their ability to lift the
hero off the ground and to transport his utopian dream
to the United Islands suggests their instrumental role
in helping him establish his individual will as he
strives to achieve his beautiful ideal. Unlike Tolya
and Lenya, who stay behind when Login embarks upon his
new life in *Bad Dreams*, the quiet children and Kirsha

accompany Trirodov, implying their constant usefulness in
the protagonist's strivings. In order to appreciate the
extent to which *A Legend in Creation* reflects Sologub's
philosophical evolution and essential optimism, one needs
to understand that Trirodov's escapist-oriented activity
represents less a rejection or total abandonment of reality than the utilization of it for higher purposes.

Such positive elements are not to be found in the
story line of the trilogy's second volume, *Queen Ortruda*.
However, here, too, it is the function of the child and
the specific nature of the protagonist's relationship to
him which mirror the writer's predominant philosophical
position. In this novel the Queen's beloved page,
Astolf, reflects the theme of escape—not through regeneration of life, but rather through its termination.
With his connection to the idea of the victory of death,
the child represents a repudiation of his counterpart's
positive role in the work's outer, Trirodov-dominated
sections. The structural position of such a thematic in-
version, coming as it does in the middle of the trilogy,
is significant in that it offers a philosophical alternative to the first volume of *A Legend in Creation*—which
will be categorically rejected in the work's last tome.

The relationship between Ortruda and Astolf is a
study in a growing, and eventually tragic, disillusion-
ment with beauty. In many respects, this sequence is a
repetition and continuation of the Sasha-Ludmila episode
in *The Petty Demon*, with Sasha's pagan boy-god status
being replaced by Astolf's identification with the "white
king" of death. Revealing a similar mixture of boyish-
ness and adult passion, which is present in Sasha Pylnikov, Astolf becomes more involved with Ortruda, and she
with him, until their all-consuming desire drives them
to murder and suicide. Both eventually realize the demise of their beautiful ideal; he, by understanding that
his increasingly erotic enjoyment of the queen's body has
led him to kill her unfaithful husband's lover, Margarita;
she, by acknowledging the boy's spiritual degeneration as
well as her own responsibility for it. A parallel situation exists in Sologub's novel *Sweeter Than Poison*,
insofar as the heroine, Shanya, also comes to discover
that the beautiful dream of her childhood lover, Zhenya,
is false. Gornfeld's observation that "Šanya had to die
because her dream was too earthly,"[44] could apply equally
to the pair of lovers in *Queen Ortruda*. Since they
recognize beauty only in its passionate and therefore

ephemeral aspect, the two can only become disappointed in
it, as their suicides attest. Even more so than in Ludmila's case, sensual desire underlies Ortruda's quest for
a more ennobling form of existence, and it is this purely
earthly phenomenon which ultimately causes the termination of her dream. To state the problem in Andrew
Field's terms, "by Ortruda's death Sologub ... signifies
the defeat of the erotic and the sensual as an alternative to the repulsiveness of ordinary life."[45] Through
her activity with Astolf, which represents an intensifi-
cation of the erotically colored relationship between
Ludmila and Sasha, it becomes clear that Sologub dis-
misses the cult of sensuality and suicide as an acceptable counterweight to a disappointing material reality.
Ortruda is the present Queen; her relationship to the
child demonstrates the lure of temporary passionate desire and the consequential "sting of death." Trirodov,
however, is the future King; his attitude toward children reveals his attraction to creative fantasy and to
the more permanent ideal of created beauty. Sologub
places the crucial words, "One must live, dream, and
create—but one does not have to live on this earth"
(XIX, 320), in Astolf's mouth. With the first half of
this statement Trirodov fully agrees. But the second
part Sologub's major spokesman reverses, and the result
constitutes the overriding philosophy of the trilogy.
For Trirodov proves in his devotion to absolute beauty—
a devotion which is based upon a commitment to beauty's
constant creation and reproduction rather than on sensuous desire and erotic body-worship—that the ideal can,
if one believes it can, be found in man's own life.

     Chukovsky pinpoints an undeniable quality in the de-
piction of the quiet children when he emphasizes the
grave-like aura which surrounds them. Often in Sologub
the concept of beauty is translated into a state of
changelessness, a sense of quietude and calm, relayed in
a setting where the subdued colors and hushed atmosphere
of a cool moonlit night predominate. But to refer to the
whole of *A Legend in Creation* as a "sepulchral novel,"[46]
as Chukovsky does, is to misunderstand the positive function of Sologub's fantastic creations, as well as the optimism which frequently underlies the work. Such a conclusion is almost inevitable if one eschews a stylistic
analysis of the book, ignoring the poetry and magic of
the language which Sologub employs to express his upbeat
mood. The true distinction between the ordinary earthly

and the beautifully rapturous, especially in Sologub's
novels, is often most strongly conveyed on the linguistic
level. Otherwise stated, whatever beauty concrete reality lacks, Sologub finds in the special quality of language itself; in its lively rhythms and enchanting
sounds. And to the extent that those sections where
children appear are the ones which are largely marked by
a uniquely lyrical and rhetorically expansive prose,
these characters can be said to be reliable indicators
of the various books' stylistic dissimilarities.

Zamyatin observed the implications which Sologub's
conception of a dual-levelled reality had on the language and diction of his writing. "Sologub," he argued,
"deliberately mixes the strongest extract of everyday
language with the elevated and refined diction of the
romantic."[47]   The style of a representative passage of
rhythmic prose from *A Legend in Creation*, which describes
Egorka's visit to the colony of the quiet children, reinforces the novel's central idea that poetry and beauty
are higher than life. The poetic diction of this section, with its alliteration, internal rhymes, syntactic
parallelisms, and repetitions, contrasts sharply with the
more neutral style which Sologub employs when depicting
scenes of ordinary life. Hardly sepulchral in tone, it
recreates, by its musical effect, a beautiful world of
wonder and enchantment.

> Uvlekali, čarovali, laskali. Poka-
> zali emu vse lesnye diva, pod peneč-
> kami, kustočkami, pod suxymi list-
> očkami nežitej lesnyx malen'kix s
> golosočkami šelestinnymi s volos-
> očkami pautinnymi - prjamen'kix i
> gorbaten'-kix, - lesnyx staričkov -
> posledyšej i poputnikov - zoev peres-
> mešnikov v kaftanax zelen'kix -
> polunočnikov i poludnevnikov, černyx
> i seryx, - žutikov-šutikov s cepkimi
> lapkami - nevidannyx ptic i zverej, -
> vse, čego net v dnevnom, zemnom,
> temnom mire.

> They lured, enchanged, and caressed (him).
> They showed him all of the forest's wonders
> under the tree-stumps, the bushes, the dry
> leaves—little wood-sprites with rustling

little voices, with spider-webby hair; little
old men of the wood—both the erect and the
hunchbacked ones; the shadow-sprites and little
companion spirits; bantering little sprites
in green coats, midnight ones and daylight
ones, grey ones and black ones; little jokers-
pokers with shaggy little paws; fabulous
birds and animals—everything that is not
to be seen in the gloomy, everyday, earthly
world (XVIII, 226).

In her stylistic investigation of Sologub as a short
story writer, Carola Hansson speaks of two languages in
Sologub's prose, and the above cited extract exemplifies
her second category:

The 'realism' of everyday reality is manifested
in a neutral, objective, matter-of-fact language... The higher reality, 'symbolism,' is
manifested in a subjective, lyrical, concen-
trated language. Sentences are organized
according to various rhythmical principles.
Inversions are common, sound orchestration
plays an important role, and words often lose
their direct referential function.[48]

There is, of course, a relationship between the
shift in the stylistic level of *A Legend in Creation*
and the theme of escape, which the child invariably
signals. Language itself functions as a primary means
of flight from routine *poshlost*. It would seem that the
writer's dependence upon rhythm becomes a device which
accomplishes stylistically what he seeks on the philosophical plane. Indeed, when scrutinizing Sologub's
prose it becomes clear that the "success" of a particular philosophical position is of secondary importance
when considered alongside the more important linguistic
dimension of his writing: Sologub is primarily and consistently a major stylist. All the more reason, then,
to question Dolinin's insistence upon Sologub's inability to excite the reader because of the "monotonality
and premeditated coldness"[49] of his writing. It is
Dikman's conclusion about Sologub's poetry which more
accurately characterizes the stylistic quality of the
fiction which we have explored. She writes that "the
harmony of (Sologub's) verse opposes evil and disharmoni-

ous reality and artistically overcomes it."[50]   Indeed,
not only in the characterization of the child, but also
in the very language which he uses to depict him, Sologub offers a world that is more wondrous and magical to
offset the drabness and dull regularity of the everyday.
In Sologub, words themselves have the power to transport
man to higher levels, to the "music of the spheres"; they
produce an enchantment which destroys routine patterns
and creates in their stead the unusual and extraordinary.
Bely experienced the hypnotic effect of Sologub's language when, as we recall, he confessed: "In your works
... there is a special note which gives them an unanalyz-
able charm.... You hypnotize (the reader) ... and one
must contend with you. I, at any rate, have struggled
with the *magic* of your words." As Trirodov with his
fantastic children, so Sologub through his magic words,
creates from the ordinary and familiar a transcendent
world of poetry and beauty.

NOTES

[1]For a discussion of Sologub's use of real people
and events in his fiction, see B. Ul'janovskaja, "O
prototipax romana F. Sologuba, *Melkij bes*," *Russkaja
literatura*, 3 (1969), pp. 181-184.
    [2]Harry Levin, *James Joyce* (New York: New Directions,
1960), p. 3.
    [3]A particularly useful book on the major literary
movements of the late nineteenth and early twentieth
centuries is *Realism, Naturalism, and Symbolism: Modes
of Thought and Expression in Europe, 1848-1914*, ed.
Roland N. Stromberg (New York: Harper and Row), 1968.
    [4]M. Dikman, op. cit., p. 17.
    [5]Ibid., p. 17.
    [6]A. Belyj, "Dalaj-lama iz Sapožka," p. 64.
    [7]A. Gornfel'd, op. cit., pp. 16-17.
    [8]W. Rowe, *Dostoevsky: Child and Man in His Works*
(New York: New York University Press, 1965), p. 71. As
a matter of fact, Sologub's voluminous notebooks to *Bad
Dreams* (housed in the Gosudarstvennaja biblioteka imeni
Saltykova-Ščedrina in Leningrad), testify to the writer's interest in the physiological sketch. Scores of
extended journalistic-like descriptions of various phenomena were originally woven into the narrative but were
subsequently removed. They remain in the notebooks—
scribbled in the margins and appended to various

sections of the text.

[9]Donald Fanger, *Dostoevsky and Romantic Realism*
(Chicago: University of Chicago Press, 1967), p. 211.

[10]F. Sologub, Letter to V. M. Latyšev, Sept. 8,
1887. Quoted in M. Dikman, op. cit., p. 12.

[11]For a discussion of Sologub's relation to the
1880s, "the epoch of social philistinism," see Ivanov-
Razumnik's *O smysle žizni*, especially pp. 40-41.

[12]F. Sologub, Letter to L. Ja. Gurevič, Nov. 15,
1895, in *Ežegodnik rukopisnogo otdela Puškinskogo Doma*,
1972, p. 119.

[13]F. Dostoevskij, *Polnoe sobranie sočinenij* (Leningrad, 1973), VI 146.

[14]Ibid., pp. 149-150

[15]M. Gofman, *Kniga o russkix pisateljax*, p. 25.

[16]Belyj, "Dalaj-lama iz Sapožka," p. 64.

[17]K. Čukovskij, "Nav'ji čary Melkogo besa," in A. N.
Čebotarevskaja, ed., *O Fedore Sologube*, p. 35.

[18]I. Mašbac-Verov, *Russkij simvolizm i put' Aleksandra Bloka* (Kujbyšev, 1969), p. 314.

[19]A. Belyj, "Dalaj-lama iz Sapožka," p. 64.

[20]Ivanov-Razumnik, op. cit., p. 49.

[21]F. Sologub, "Iskusstvo našix dnej," p. 51.

[22]V. Ivanov, "Rasskazy tajnovidca," *Vesy*, 8 (1904),
p. 50.

[23]A. Gornfel'd, op. cit., p. 51.

[24]"Ėllis," *Russkie simvolisty* (Moscow, 1910), p. 2.

[25]E. Zamjatin, op. cit., p. 36.

[26]A. Gornfel'd, *Knigi i ljudi* (St. Petersburg,
1908), p. 39.

[27]A. Dolinin, op. cit., p. 61.

[28]F. M. Dostoevskij, Letter to N. N. Straxov (March,
1869). Quoted in R. L. Jackson, *Dostoevsky's Quest for
Form* (New Haven: Yale University Press, 1966), p. 82.

[29]F. M. Dostoevskij, Letter to I.S. Turgenev (Dec.,
1863). Quoted in R. L. Jackson, op. cit., p. 81.

[30]E. Zamjatin, op. cit., p. 36.

[31]These are the first lines of a poem which Sologub
wrote in 1907, and *A Legend in Creation* represents the
fullest realization of their meaning. In this trilogy
Sologub demonstrates his belief in the "eternal return,"
specifically by resurrecting characters from other
novels (e.g., Molin from *Bad Dreams*; Peredonov from *The
Petty Demon*), as well as by depicting scenes in which
the dead return to earth in their previously recognizable
forms.

[32] A. Field, "The Created Legend: Sologub's Symbolic Universe," *Slavic and East European Journal*, V (1961), p. 348.

[33] D. S. Mirsky makes this point in his brief discussion of the work. See Mirsky, op. cit., p. 445.

[34] J. Holthusen, *Fedor Sologubs Roman Trilogie (Tvorimaja legenda)* (The Hague, 1960), p. 33.

[35] F. M. Dostoevskij, *Sobranie sočinenij v 10 tomax* (Moscow, 1958), 434.

[36] J. Holthusen, op. cit., p. 52.

[37] The journey to the moon by spaceship is a theme found in the fiction of H. G. Wells, whose works Sologub knew very well. Sologub displayed an interest in utopian/fantastic literature from the very beginning of his career, as evidenced in his mention in *Bad Dreams* of Edward Bellamy's *Looking Backward*.

[38] K. Čukovskij, "Putevoditel' po Sologubu," p. 360.

[39] Ibid., p. 360.

[40] F. Sologub, "Mečta preobraženija" (1915). Quoted in Dikman, op. cit., p. 42. Dikman does not mention the original place of publication of Sologub's article.

[41] J. Holthusen, op. cit., p. 24.

[42] Helen Muchnic, *Russian Writers: Notes and Essays* (New York: Random House, 1971), p. 221.

[43] "Iskusstvo našix dnej," p. 47, my emphasis.

[44] A. Gornfel'd, op. cit., p. 52.

[45] A. Field, op. cit., p. 347.

[46] K. Čukovskij, "Putevoditel' po Sologubu," p. 358.

[47] E. Zamjatin, op. cit., p. 36.

[48] C. Hansson, *Fedor Sologub as a Short-Story Writer: Stylistic Analyses* (Stockholm: Almquist and Wiksell, 1975), p. 19.

[49] A. Dolinin, op. cit., p. 58.

[50] M. Dikman, op. cit., p. 56.

CHAPTER IV

THE FAIRY TALES

The theme of the creative and redemptive power of language becomes ever important in Sologub's *oeuvre* and the child's particular relationship to it is most evident in the writer's *Fairy Tales (Skazki)*. Prolific author that he was, Sologub utilized a wide variety of literary genres—the short story, the novella, the novel, the play, the lyric poem, the literary-philosophical essay, and, under the influence of Russia's rich folkloric tradition, the fairy tale. The year 1905 saw the publication of his *Book of Fairy Tales (Kniga skazok)*, which was followed a year later by the *Political Fairy Tales (Politicheskie skazochki)*, a slim volume of fifty pages, roughly two thirds the length of its predecessor. Most of Volume Ten of the *Collected Works*—nearly one hundred and twenty pages—is devoted to over seventy of these tales which Sologub gathered under the heading of "Skazochki" and which we shall study in this chapter.

It is neither accidental nor surprising that Sologub's interest in folklore should surface at the dawn of what was to be an undeniably optimistic shift in his world view, commencing in full force with his embarkment upon *A Legend in Creation* in 1907. The different varieties of folk genres, with their strong orientation toward the marvelous and the mythic, accord very well with the writer's exploration of new and more positive forms of escape, his emphasis upon the need to transform reality, and his attraction to increasingly nonrealist strains in his art.[1] Indeed, among the writer's most original literary creations, the fairy tales best embody the legend and most effectively convey the special mood of fantasy of which Sologub's novel—trilogy later speaks. In a broader sense, Sologub's literary use of folkloric material reflects the symbolists' interest in otherness and their desire to discover and create higher, more perfect forms of existence. A period which saw numerous attempts to obliterate the borders between utopia and reality, the years which directly preceded the Bolshevik Revolution produced many writers whose consciousness was sharply focused both on the possibility of adapting fairy tales to their own work, as well as on the peculiar ideology or *Weltanschauung* which the fairy tale world presupposes.

After, and perhaps inspired by, Sologub, writers such as
Alexey Remizov (1877-1957) and Velimir Khlebnikov (1885-
1922) also depended upon the folk or fairy tale as a major form of literary expression.

If, as Roger Sale and others argue,[2] a major characteristic of the fairy tale is its deliberate attempt *not*
to convey reality, *not* to distinguish real from unreal or
separate fantasy from fact, then Sologub's "skazočki" fit
squarely into this category. Roughly one third of the
tales employ the major nonrealistic device of animals or
inanimate objects that talk or in other ways act like human beings. Like the opening piece, "The Hammer and the
Chain" ("Molot i cep'"), which relates how the two dis-
cuss such matters as freedom and slavery, these tales re-
quire that adult logic be suspended. We are fully in an
irrational world where thinking is animistic and where
animate and inanimate, human and nonhuman, are treated
alike. The result, as we expect in fairy tales, is a
model of reality which is as wondrous and magical as it
is simple and uncomplicated, primarily because even the
most unusual or disturbing events are presented in an
easy, casual style and are elevated by the prevailing
tone of enchantment.

In "The Traveller Stone" ("Putešestvennik kamen'"),
a pebble that is thrown into the window of a house and is
then tossed out, brags to the other stones on the pave-
ment about how wonderful the experience of living among
people was, but lies when it expresses love of the "simple folk" as the reason for its return. A discussion between "The Key and the Lock Pick" ("Ključ i otmyčka")
concludes with the moral that the key is better off being
honest, if inactive, than the lock pick, which is active
but dishonest and which lacks any conception of truth and
loyalty. In "The Frogs" ("Ljaguški"), which recalls the
genre of animal fable both in its humor and in its obvious reference to the human sphere with all of its weak-
nesses, the Russian frog is quick to criticize others
(his French peers) for his own shortcomings (his inability to croak in French). The main character in "The
Crayfish Moves Backwards" ("Rak pjatitsja nazad") turns
out to be smarter than his would-be captors give him
credit for, as they explain his ingenuity via a lovely
play on words: "Xvost-to u nego *speredi*, a golova s
glazami *szadi*—tol'ko *pered* s xvostom u nego *szadi*, a *zad*
s golovoju *speredi*." ("He has his tail in *front* and his
head and eyes *at the back*—only his *front* (part) with his

tail is *in the back* (quarters) with his head in the
front," X, 107). In "The Wand" ("Paločka") we are told
of a wondrous stick which transforms everything into a
remote dream and allows for constant renewal and happiness. This tale is one of Sologub's shortest (ten
lines) and most charming and, if one allows that the
fairy tale itself works like the wand, the piece explains
Sologub's particular fascination for the genre.

> Est' takaja čudesnaja paločka na svete—
> k čemu by ni kosnis', vse totčas delaetsja snom,
> i propadaet.
> Vot esli tebe ne nravitsja tvoja žizn', voz'mi
> paločku, prižmi ee koncom k svoej golove—i
> vdrug uvidiš' čto vse bylo snom, i staneš' opjat'
> žit' snačala i sovsem po inomu.
> A čto bylo ran'se, v ètom sne, pro vse vovse
> zabudeš'.
> Vot kakaja est' čudesnaja na svete paločka.

> There is a certain miraculous wand and what-
> ever it touches is immediately turned into
> a dream and disappears.
> For instance, if your life is unpleasant, take
> the wand, press one of its ends against your
> head—and you'll immediately see that all was a
> dream, and once again you'll live anew and
> completely differently.
> And what existed previously, in this dream,
> will be totally forgotten.
> That's the kind of miraculous wand that exists.
> (X, 43)

In Sologub's hands the fairy tale has the power to
turn even harsh reality into something beautiful and up-
lifting. These tales, like most others in Sologub's
collection, are parables, pithy statements or anecdotes,
which most often stress action and contain dialogue as
opposed to straight description. They are rendered
charming, as fairy tales tend to be, by their attempt to
efface all distinctions between objects and animate
beings, to attune us to the special relationship which
exists among all things, and to present a world of un-
limited possibilities where the fantastic is as unexceptional as the everyday. Here it is perfectly legitimate,
say, for "A Bird-Cherry Blossom and A Skunk" ("Čeremuxa i

vonjučka") to argue about who has the right to smell.
Everything is alive by virtue of the particular quality
which defines it; the blossom's emission of sweet perfume, like the skunk's discharge of a foul odor, endows
each with a will, a personality of its own such that
their ability to communicate is not at all unnatural. The
world of the fairy tale is a self-enclosed one, the frame
of reference is the tale itself and not the events of external reality. Thus, physical settings are general and
action occurs "in a certain time, at a certain place."
Only once in the entire collection is a locale readily
identifiable: the Nevsky Prospect, in "The Little Ray of
Sun in the Dungeon" ("Lučiška v temničke"). Taken on its
own terms, then, we can accept or believe even a tale's
most miraculous phenomena.

Such is not the case in many of Sologub's stories
where, so to speak, fantastic content is related in logical form. A realist perspective predominates in the latter works and the identical presence of supernatural elements often imparts a sense of the unbelievable and
ludicrous, forcing us to reject the subject matter as
silly. A case in point is the description of the young
boy Serezhka's affection for a birch tree in "The White
Birch," which concludes with their final embrace as they
perish together. The story relates Serezhka's infatu-
ation for the nearby birch because he is convinced that
it alone understands his alienation from life's hostile
elements. Yet the communication between the two, which
would be perfectly natural in the genre of fairy tale,
is unacceptable in the short story mode. The boy's dec-
laration, made in perfectly grown-up language, that "I
love you because you are springlike, because you have
grown for my delight" (XII, 17), sounds silly. Unlike
the more successful fairy tales, "The White Birch" presents the illogical and fantastic in a rational, adult,
and deadly serious manner and it is such incongruity
which causes our resistance to believe in its validity.

The aura of magic and enchantment, which we have
mentioned, constitutes perhaps the clearest reason, the
most immediate evidence for the rightful inclusion of
Sologub's *skazki* in the genre of fairy tale. But they
fit into the tradition in other ways, especially in
their possession of certain linguistic features which
betray a clearly folkloric, oral influence. The fairy
tale, as Jakobson,[3] among others, has shown, was initially an oral production; it was the property of tellers

of tales who originated among and performed for the common folk, before it was adopted by writers and absorbed
into the written tradition, beginning, in Russia's case,
in the eighteenth century. The very root of the word in
Russian indicates the genre's oral nature, for "skaz" in
the modern parlance as well, means telling or saying.
Much to the credit of Sologub's linguistic skills, the
authenticity of the fairy tales stems from their reten-
tion of what Mirsky calls the "verbal effects"[4] of the
popular language.

The use of pairs of words with practically the same
meaning, a common device of the folk or fairy tale, is
prevalent in Sologub's collection as well: almost half of
the works begin with the stock opening "žili byli"
("there once lived") or simply with "žil." Nor is it
unusual to find combinations such as "vernulsja xorošij
mal'čik domoj, i stal *žit'-poživat'* po xorošemu" ("the
boy returned home and began *to live* well"). Repetition
and alliteration are also common: two examples of the
former are "*šel, šel* belyj čelovek, i *prišel* v korobku"
("Kolodki i petli," "Boottrees and Buttonholes") and
"*parilsja, parilsja, zaparilsja,* umer po polke ...
kričala, kričala, zakričalas', umerla po galerke" ("Xryč
da xryčevka," "The Old Fogey and His Wife"). An example
of the latter is "*mal'čik s pal'čik* vstretil mal'čika s
nogotok..." ("Obidčiki," "The Offenders"). Less frequent, but also a basic folkloric device, is the attribu-
tive use of adjectives in the short form, for example
"krasna devočka" in "Kryl'ja" ("Wings").

Yet for all the crucial points of intersection between Sologub's fairy tales and the typical representatives of this genre, his tales contain a special quality,
they exude a certain magic, a particular kind of poetry
which set them apart as works of a highly original order.
Sologub's writing attempts, and often successfully, to
follow Trirodov's injunction in Part One of *A Legend in
Creation*, that art, first and foremost, say or achieve
something new. Many of Sologub's stories contribute a
different dimension to the genre by capturing the complex and troubled mood during the crisis of adolescent
sexuality. *The Petty Demon* and *A Legend in Creation* ex-
pand the territory of novelistic inquiry by conjuring up
a world of unforgettable characters and events, each related in a style eminently suited to the subject at
hand. The *Fairy Tales* work within an old and established
tradition but move beyond it to achieve a singular

effect. Indeed, to examine the idiosyncratic nature of
these pieces is to discover the writer's peculiar understanding of this mode and his attempt to employ its
aesthetic and philosophical potential in new ways.

Curiously downplayed in Sologub's fairy tale world
are some of the principal sources of its customary wonder: magic potions and objects, dwarfs, dragons, witches,
kings, queens, princes and princesses, and the like. In
this collection of over seventy *skazki*, only a handful
contains characters who are stock figures in the fairy or
magical tale proper (in Russian, "volšebnaja skazka").

This phenomenon immediately signals the specialness
of Sologub's fairy tales. In a mode which is usually
reserved for the most supernatural and exotic, which is
ordinarily the furthest removed from everyday locales as
it transports the reader to far-away places inhabited by
exceptional beings, Sologub is curiously earthly, unex-
pectedly local in orientation. The magic is there in
full; the remoteness, however, is kept to a minimum. And
this is exactly the point, for to achieve the dream-like
aura which pervades the wondrous fairy tale realm, Sologub need not go further than present reality with its
mundane events. He can, and seeks to, derive the miraculous from the here and now; he is able to find it in the
special status of childhood, as we recall him writing:

> I pervoe čudo na svete,
> Velikij istočnik utex—
> Blaženno-nevinnye deti,
> Ix sladkij i radostnyj smex.

> And the foremost miracle on earth,
> The greatest source of delight—
> Are blessedly innocent children,
> Their sweet and joyful laughter.

As Trirodov creates a fantastic order of "quiet children" from perfectly natural and everyday creatures such
as Egorka, so Sologub constructs an enchanted universe
solely by reproducing the unique perspective of the
child. Enchantment here depends less on the presence of
fantastic places, objects, or creatures than it does on
the freshness, purity, and lovely wonderment of the
child's outlook. At its most essential, fairy tale in
Sologub is synonymous with seeing the world through the
child's eye. Magic is attained through imaginative

vision and no one possesses it more than children.

This is the message of "Fairy Tales in Flower Beds and Fairy Tales in the Palace" ("Skazki na grjadkax i skazki vo dvorce"), the only tale in the collection which uses the word "skazki" repeatedly and for significant purposes. A gardener's son is fascinated by the beautiful fairy tales which grow on the tsaritsa's grounds—white, red, blue, lilac, and yellow. Word about them spreads from the little boy to his friends and their families (none of whom may enter these private gardens), to the ruler herself, who shows interest in the phenomenon and has some samples brought to her palace for inspection. "The tsaritsa looked at the fairy tales, expressed surprise and said: 'What is so interesting about them? What kind of fairy tales are these? They are just simple flowers.' And the poor fairy tales were thrown out of the window and the gardener's little son was soundly thrashed for saying such silly things" (X, 62). The child's eyes see the flowers as dreams or tales which represent a different reality; to his imagination they contain a rare and special essence. To the adult, however, who knows only everyday reality and who can no longer believe in fairy tales and the magic they presuppose, these specimens are judged literally, as "just simple flowers." The child's imaginative flights are countered by some hard, sobering blows, yet victory does not belong to the adult world, for it is the child's perspective which predominates.

Content alone is not the crucial element in Sologub's fairy tales; equally important is the form. If this were not so, our response to "Fairy Tales in Flower Beds and Fairy Tales in the Palace" would be identical to the one we experience when reading, say, Sologub's story "Dream on the Stones," whose title, not to mention subject matter, approximates the similar opposition between fantasy (the flower beds) and reality (the palace) of the tale. Both pieces conclude with the adult's destruction of the youngster's special world. But its brightness and purity are maintained in the fairy tale, and thus a happy end guaranteed, precisely through the point of view, which is the child's throughout. Unlike the story, the tale is narrated exclusively from this point of view. Its beginning, "there was a garden in which fairy tales grew in beds along the road," takes the miraculous for granted and, as fairy tales do, expresses the fantastic in a perfectly natural and factual manner. But more importantly,

its conclusion—even after the child's world is allegedly
shattered—sustains this magic. The tsaritsa sees
through these "fairy tales," but only she calls them
flowers and when, directly preceding the child's beating,
she throws them out of the window, they are still called
"skazki." As is so often true in Sologub's fairy tales,
the form—the mode of narration—provides a charming
tonality, a happy conclusion to the subject matter, which
is not, unlike traditional examples of the genre, necessarily joyous. Even the title of the present piece, with
its syntactic parallelism and repetition of the word
"skazki," provides a light, poetic cast as opposed to the
more neutral wording of its short story counterpart,
"Dream on the Stones." As will soon become evident, the
idea that language itself can transform the world, that
it can create its own reality and effect the attitudes we
have toward it, is a crucial one in the *Fairy Tales*.

Of course, the association of the fairy tale with
children is hardly surprising. After all, while most
representatives of the genre, Sologub's included, are not
written for a juvenile audience, the mode of thinking
which they evoke is often and quite naturally connected
to the child's peculiarly animistic or primitive view of
reality, to his tendency toward an irrational, more out-
wardly fantastic outlook on life. Sologub's innovativeness lies in his combination of these two components—the
genre and the person whom it most readily brings to mind.
That is to say, Sologub "localizes" the fairy tale, applying it to the age group to which, in some senses, it
most naturally belongs. Alone among Russian writers who
had previously adapted the genre to their work—Pushkin,
Gogol, Leskov, Saltykov-Schedrin and Tolstoy, to name the
major ones—Sologub does more than *imply* the uniqueness
of the child's frame of thinking in his fairy tales. He
actually populates them largely with these characters
(roughly half of them contain children), and shows how
the child's mere everyday experience is the most wondrous, the most fairy-tale like form of existence.

Sologub introduces us to the child's bright and joyous private realm, to his games, rituals, dreams, special
objects, and even his pranks. "The Merry Girl"
("Veselaja devčonka") tells of a girl who always smiles,
even when her mother threatens to hit her. The child in
"The Fruit Drop" ("Ledenčik") treasures her last piece of
candy and debates how much of it she ought to give to a
poor girl until what little is left is hardly worth

dispensing. Another tale, "Baj" relates how Manya engages in word play as she imagines the appearance of a
Central Asian landowner ("baj") on her four bedroom walls
while her nanny sings her a lullaby—which contains the
same word and triggers the association: "Baj, baj, baj,
Manju pokačaj" ("Bye, bye, bye, rock-a-bye little
Manja"). The tale is a charming combination of the
nurse's singing and the child's continued flights of
imagination—both based on the word "baj," and it ends
when, finally, Manya falls asleep. "Wings" tells how
several girls, one richer than the other and each after
the failure of the last, try to grow wings. All fail,
but on the "Wing-mother's" intercession, the poorest girl
of all, and one who has not even participated in the ef-
fort, succeeds, whereupon "she began to fly to heaven
and sing songs."

In the above examples and even in unexceptional
tales which relate no more than a brief conversation or
an interior monologue devoid of any plot or drama, the
mere presence of the child, with his disarming simplicity, straightforwardness, and freshness of perspective,
endows the situation with a special effect. Here the
relationship of the reader to the fairy tale recalls the
attitude of the gardener's son to the flowers in "Fairy
Tales in Flower Beds..."—something purely ordinary becomes the source of particular enchantment. "What Will
Be?" ("Čto budet?") provides an excellent example. This
tale merely conveys a talk between a child, who knows
what will be, and his parents, who do not. After much dialogue, which is related in riddle-like fashion, it turns
out that the child does not know what will be and can
only weep at this discovery. "And that's how the misunderstanding ended" (X, 47), concludes the piece. The
subject matter is undramatic and unexceptional but, as
stated earlier, Sologub often emphasizes form over content to achieve his desired effect in this genre. The
short, almost stacatto sentences, the uncomplicated syntax and the repetition of certain phrases, mostly beginning with the conjunction "a," ("and" or "but")—all of
which are features of the child's speech—create a sense
of simple innocence, a special kind of poetry which is
precisely the author's objective.

Indeed, when speaking of the child's role in the
Fairy Tales we mean as much his linguistic as his physical presence. Even in the tales which lack juvenile
characters, the frame of mind and the pattern of speech

which are implicit in the narration of the events are
quite often those of the child. An examination of "The
Boy and the Birch" ("Mal'čik i bereza") demonstrates
many of these linguistic features.

    V sadu rosla bereza. Na dače žil mal'čik
Nika. Nika byl šalun. A u berezy byli vetki.
Raz Nika mnogo šalil. Togda s berezy sorvali
vetku, a s vetki list'ja obdernuli.
    Potom už Nika ne ljubil berezu. Vot leto
bylo dolgo, i nastal ijul', i konec ijulja.
Na bereze pokazalis' želtye list'ja. Nika
skazal bereze:
    "Čto, zljučka, vot tebja Bog i nakazal—
drugie derev'ja molodye, a ty uže sedaja."

    A birch tree grew in a garden. The young
boy Nika was living at the summer house. Nika
was a prankster. The birch tree had branches.
Once Nika was joking around a lot. Then he tore
a branch off the birch and with it the leaves
as well.
    Then Nika didn't like the birch any more.
The summer was long, and July arrived and then
the end of July. The birch had yellow leaves
on it. Nika said to the birch:
    "See, you nasty thing, God has punished you—
the other trees are young and you're already
gray." (X, 17)

    The sentences tend to be extremely short, often con-
sisting of three or four words, and the syntax uncomplicated. Occasional run-on sentences or repetitiveness
exist ("i nastal ijul', i konec ijulja"). But more
prevalent are the large numbers of particles, conjunc-
tions, and interjections which capture the child's sense
of dramatic rhetoric by conveying naive wonderment over,
or particular emphasis upon, a phenomenon ("Vot leto
bylo dolgo"). The preponderance of oppositions, the
tendency to see things in simple categories of black and
white, or to look at the world solely in terms of "I"
and "you" or "mine" and "yours," behavior which is frequently associated with children, finds reinforcement on
the linguistic level. The title alone of this tale, as
well as the majority already cited, illustrates the important emphasis on contrasts, as does the frequent use

of the conjunction "a" in the sense of "but": e.g.,
"drugie derev'ja molodye, a ty uže sedaja." One gets the
impression in these numerous cases of the desire to iso-
late objects into separate camps, to distinguish them
according to specific features—often with the egocentric
and recognizably childlike motive of calling attention to
one's own autonomy or individuality.

The colloquial and diminutive form "zljučka" should
not go unnoticed because the inordinate number of such
words in the *Fairy Tales* especially signals the child's
presence. We are squarely in the world of miniatures,
both in terms of the size of the tales—which average
about a page in length—and the high frequency of dimin-
utives which, again, is a linguistic feature associated
with children. One encounters diminutive forms (e.g.,
dumočka, odežka, šapočka, glazen'ki) virtually on every
page, but what merits particular attention is the sense
of familiarity which these words impart and the feeling
of warmth which they convey. The title of the collection, "Skazočki," is itself a diminutive and it establishes from the outset the light tone and playful, joyous mood which Sologub attempts to produce here.

Rhyme also contributes to this mood; we find it in
characters' names, such as "Maška-zamaraška," but even
more so in the titles of the tales: "Paločka pogonjaločka
i šapočka mnogodumočka," "Lučiška v temničke," "Frica
iz-za granicy," to name a few. And there is even a case
where it would seem that the *raison d'etre* of an entire
tale is simply the creation of its final rhyme. "Spatinki" ("Sleeping spirits," again a colloquial, diminutive
form) tells how Volya falls asleep in mid-day and is
prevented from doing his work. He is found by his nanny
and led home, as she warns: "Ne spi, *Volja, v pole,*
lučše spatinki doma." ("Don't sleep, Volya, in the
field; sleeping spirits are better dealt with at home").

We are, in Sologub's *Fairy Tales*, midway between
poetry and prose. The colloquialisms, the use of conversation, of paired words and alliteration, yield a
texture which is less "refined" and literary in nature
and one which more faithfully approximates the oral,
folk-poetic style. But the collection attains to poetry
in other ways. The compactness, intensity, and imaginativeness of the language, the lovely, lilting quality of
the "young" diction, the wonderful way Sologub gives
life to words as he conveys them through the prism of
the child's psychic apparatus, and the brevity of the

tales, which almost *look* like verse on the printed page—
all of this contributes to what is surely an ingenious
linguistic performance. Jakobson has insisted that "the
originality of the Russian fairy tale lies not in plot
but ... in its stylistic adornments,"[5] and Sologub's
fairy tales admirably adhere to this tradition.

Given this poetic originality, the political overtones which some of Sologub's fairy tales possess reveal
even more convincingly the subtle and delicate hand of a
major talent. Sologub did not distinguish between his
political and nonpolitical fairy tales when republishing
them in his *Collected Works*, although roughly the last
third of Volume Ten consists of those pieces which had
previously appeared under the heading of *Political Tales*.
These tales are especially noteworthy for the way in
which their pleasant form contains, and almost conceals,
their bitter, even scathing content. At least initially
these works are deceptively innocent because their harsh
sociopolitical criticism lies embedded beneath the simplicity and charm of their language.

"Extra Rope" ("Lišnye verevočki") relates how two
strict parents decide to tie up their naughty child,
despite his efforts to restrain himself. They punish
and even jeer at him, believing that these acts will
help him forget how to misbehave. The parents intensify
this regime and tie the boy even tighter after their
window is broken one night and they find a note which
protests their treatment of the boy. But when this act
is repeated a second time, accompanied by a threat to
break all the windows, the couple becomes fearful and
tries to placate any hostile opinions of them. They
visit their neighbors and announce that they are removing the extra rope with which they had bound the child
after the first rock-throwing incident. Now the couple
sleeps soundly, thinking that no one will touch them.

The child is a convenient device to represent, as
he does in the other prose genres, an innocent victim of
harsh and arbitrary uses of authority. Many of Sologub's
fairy tales, political and nonpolitical, depict children
who are pitted against mean and forceful parents. With
their crude methods and their misunderstanding of the
child's natural behavior, the adults can be seen, in
sociopolitical terms, as a repressive government which
mishandles its subjects. Troubled by growing unrest
(the stone-throwing incidents), and concerned with public opinion (their visits to local parents), the vic-

timizers relent by relaxing some of their control, although by no means allowing their victim his necessary
freedom. But for them even a slight loosening of their
grip is a significant concession, and the tale ends with
their new (albeit false) sense of security.

"Extra Rope" exhibits the causticness and biting
sarcasm found in the best examples of Saltykov-Schedrin's
popular sociopolitical *Fairy Tales* (1880–1885), which
Sologub obviously knew and emulated. However, Sologub's
counterparts, because they are conveyed as if through
the child's perspective, exude that special fragrance of
which we have spoken above and are thus more akin to
pure poetry. The poet Maksimilian Voloshin makes this
point and places these works in their proper literary
context when he insists that "Sologub's fairy tales are
the historical bridge between the contemporary understanding of the fairy tale and Schedrin's tales."[6]
"Contemporary understanding" is meant to signify the
freedom of the genre from its obligation to relate a
story so that it may concentrate more heavily on the
tale's stylistic potential and the mentality of its
teller.

And indeed one can appreciate even Sologub's political fairy tales solely as brilliant verbal perform-
ances, for one tends to assess their subject matter only
after marveling at their linguistic effects, which no
translation can convey. The writer himself seemingly
und rstood this when he decided to efface their political distinction by removing the title from his later compilation in the *Collected Works*. Many of Sologub's
other fairy tales could be read in such a way as to
qualify for inclusion into the last third of the volume,
although they were not published as "political" pieces
originally. What ultimately unites all the fairy tales,
what constitutes their lowest common denominator, is
their sheer poetic beauty. This is all the more reason
why it is so difficult to agree with Dolinin's generalization that Sologub's style is marked by "its monotony,
by its unusually severe finish, and by what I would say
is its rather deliberate coldness."[7] A proper reading
of the *Fairy Tales* should permanently set to rest the
long-held fallacy that Sologub's artistic universe possesses a singularly sluggish, static, and lifeless quality.

As the *Political Fairy Tales* demonstrate, words
such as "simple" and "miniature" may describe the form

of Sologub's works in this genre, but they do not apply
to their content, which is often grave and complex in
nature. Even less so do such words apply to the ideological position which these works hold in the overall
scheme of the writer's creative universe. Written at a
critical and transitional period in Sologub's development, the fairy tales express a central aspect of his
artistic and philosophical credo. Instead of expressing
a bleaker, more pessimistic and apocalyptic tone after
the dismal failure of the Revolution of 1905, Sologub
gradually turned away from his previously gloomy outlook
to a more positive and upbeat one. Several stories of
1908-1909 were subtitled "legends" and were published in
a volume whose title best describes the predominant, although by no means exclusive, mood of this period: *A Book
of Enchantments (Kniga očarovanij*, 1909). Reading the
twenty volume *Collected Works* in their chronological order, one readily observes that the thread which runs
through these books and binds them together is the writer's continuing search for redemption and faith. The
Fairy Tales—perhaps not accidentally the center, the
tenth volume, of the collection—commences a crucial and
more upward stage in this process, which concludes in
volumes eighteen, nineteen, and twenty—*A Legend in Creation.*

Indeed, one could argue that the fairy tales most
persuasively demonstrate the important relationship that
exists in Sologub between faith and creative imagination. Belief exists when we are able to accept the non-
real as real, when we are willing to suspend our adher-
ance to traditional physical and temporal laws and accept other forms of reality. This can be accomplished
by means of language, through the magic and power of
words and creative acts, which produce those new and
miraculous existences of which Trirodov speaks in *A
Legend in Creation.*

Two pieces in the *Fairy Tales*, "Those of the Future" ("Buduščie") and "They" ("Oni") speak lamentingly
of a higher order of pure spirit, completely unlike our
material reality and inevitably destroyed upon contact
with it. Technically these tales do not qualify for inclusion in the genre; they are closer to tone poems of a
contemplative, metaphysical nature, similar to Turgenev's
Poems in Prose (1879-1883). But each expresses a longing to experience a pure, innocent, and ecstatic existence, the sense of which Sologub produces in the very

collection to which these pieces belong. Sologub's momentary glimpse of this world in "They" leads him to explain frustratingly: "Oh, if only I were able to find the
word to describe it!" (77). One feels that the other
tales of the collection constitute such an attempt. With
their fuller agreement of narrational voice and narrative
content, the fairy tales represent the most sustained and
self-contained examples of the writer's desired world of
dream. Sologub's vision attains cosmic dimensions here,
for the entire earthly community is elevated to the more
imaginative level of poetry and fantasy. The simplest
details, the most inconsequential objects and routine
situations are transfigured, such that they occupy a more
exalted status.

        Take, for example, "A Drop of Rain and a Speck of
Dust" ("Kaplja i pylinka"). In five lines Sologub nar-
rates how a falling drop decides to merge with something
solid rather than merely swimming in a puddle. So it
joins together with a speck of dust and lies on the
ground as a ball of dirt. What we have is a trifling
phenomenon: a bit of mud on the street, explained in a
fresh and delightful manner. So it is in "The Yellowed
Birch Leaf, the Drop of Rain and the Lower Sky"
("Poželtevšij berezovyj list, kaplja i nižnee nebo").
The existence of a yellow leaf is provided a history, a
reason and, by extension, a dignity of its own. A rain-
drop falls on it and enjoys its stay, but convinced that
there is a lower sky beneath the leaf, it gladly falls
to the ground, certain that it hears the swaying branches
whispering: "lower sky." Abandoned and grief-stricken,
the birch leaf turns yellow. Once again, an ordinary
phenomenon is endowed with meaning and magic: in content, as in form, this brief incident conveys a sense of
loveliness, it achieves a uniqueness otherwise absent.
Such is the case in the above-mentioned "A Bird-Cherry
Blossom and a Skunk," which also constitutes a lovely
history, a beautiful explanation of an ordinary situation: several passers-by noting how a skunk who is sit-
ting near a bird-cherry tree interferes with the flower's aroma. They simply see the physical aspect of this
phenomenon, unaware of its larger dimensions and hidden
life—unlike the reader, who experiences it in the conversation which has just ensued between plant and animal.

        We have, then, yet another definition, a different
use, of fairy tale in Sologub. It is a means of explain-

ing the existence of mundane events and, even more so, of
imparting to them a new and more beautiful meaning and,
therefore, a higher significance. Sologub does not reject or ignore the everyday world, rather he poeticizes
it and creates from its common matter different orders of
reality. These tales are cosmogenies—each one creating
its own universe by providing original explanations of
the particular phenomenon described within it. These
phenomena and the stories about their existence are infinite, and in writing the *Fairy Tales* Sologub paves the
way for Trirodov's later statement about the need to
create many ever-changing realities.

Original as it may be, the writer's use of the fairy
tale to depict so comprehensively a romantic world of
beauty is not surprising. Traditionally the fairy tale
has always concerned itself less with the common, empirical order of everyday existence. The special charm which
is indigenous to the genre would seem more naturally to
convey Sologub's romantic craving for the miraculous.
Bryusov first realized that the fairy tales were the most
effective expression of Sologub's search for life's hidden mystery and as such the purest forms of his symbolism. This is so, he argued, not because reality disappears altogether in them but because its antithesis is
always visible beneath the surface.

The composer of sacred hymns to the star Mair,
(Sologub) at the same time wants to preserve in
the dialogues of the characters of his stories
the abusive words of everyday reality. In Sologub's bursts into the otherworldly, one always
feels a kind of heaviness of an all too earthly
body... In his *Book of Fairy Tales* both peculiarities of Sologub's work are somehow successfully combined. Reality is not intermingled
with dream, but is totally fused with it.[8]

With their obliteration of "abusive words" and their
complete romanticization of ordinary life, the *skazki*
conform to Sologub's notion, as paraphrased by Ivanov-
Razumnik, that "every genuine work of art ... should be a
combination of the 'yes' and the 'no,' of realism and
romanticism."[9] Real life and fantasy are fully inter-
twined in the fairy tales with the result that the boundary between them is effaced. Interesting is Bryusov's
perception that this is effected by language itself.

The apparent merging of dream and reality in the
Fairy Tales does not mean that the world which is presented in them is a homogenized one, purged of human
foibles. As we evidence particularly in the *Political
Fairy Tales*, man's negative impulses are every bit as
present here as they are in Sologub's prose fiction. The
content of many fairy tales speaks to the futility of
human existence in a world ruled by arbitrary fate and
inhabited by people who are limited by their selfish interests and narrow outlooks. Yet in the fairy tales the
predominant vision of life is markedly less tortured and
contradictory than in Sologub's other writing. Evil and
virtue are equally present but, unlike reality, the fairy
tale world is purged of ambiguous grey areas. Moreover,
no infraction ever attains metaphysical proportions and
the mood is thus free from what Bryusov labels as heaviness. The adult perspective, Bryusov's "all too earthly
body," disappears and with it vanishes the emotional
anguish, which many critics had accused Sologub of often
transferring unconvincingly onto his child-heroes. A
psyche which is ordinarily torn, and fully colored, by a
dualistic world view yields to a different domain. Evil
is acknowledged but only as a natural part of a much
larger universe in which optimism and enchantment still
predominate. As Bryusov understood, the fairy tales reflect to a far less significant degree than Sologub's
other writing the alternation between moments of doubt
and belief, between reality and dream. Rather, the
antipodes coalesce because the presentation of even negative, potentially agony-producing elements is filtered
through the child's wondrous, pure, and simple imagination.

Not that Sologub has any illusions about the child's
world: it is filled with acts of dishonesty, greed,
selfishness, and even violence. In "White, Gray, Black,
Red" ("Belye, serye, černye, krasnye") a spoiled child's
incendiary impulses result in a destroyed house and his
death. "Unheated Stoves" ("Netoplennye peči") tells of
some children gleefully breaking and burning their furni-
ture in order to keep warm. "Fritz From Abroad" ("Frica
iz-za granicy") relates how two bad Russian children are
exchanged for the well-behaved Fritz. The latter dies of
cholera and the two Russian children end up in German
jails. In "The Evil Boy and the Quiet Boy" ("Zloj mal'-
čik i Tixij mal'čik"), evil wins out as the innocent boy
is accused and punished. "I ego postavili v ugol, a

Zlogo mal'čika pogladili po golovke. Tak-to často
byvaet."   ("And he was put in the corner and the Evil boy
was patted on the head. That's the way it often is"). There
are no happy endings in the sense of justness or fairness
prevailing; there is often no resolution of unpleasantness, but merely the affirmation of its existence.

The lack of justice notwithstanding, the situations
in these tales never approach tragic or gloomy proportions, for the tone remains light and the language familiar and entertaining. The final sentences in the last
tale maintain a sense of casualness, even charm, despite
the sad outcome. The diminutive "golovka" scales down
the emotional as well as physical dimensions, as does the
particle "to" in "tak-to." The "to" is used simply as a
filler, but its importance lies precisely in its meaninglessness. This particle helps to diffuse a potentially
sad mood and soften what ordinarily would be bitterness
at life's injustices. Thus, the miraculous power of
words removes, or at least minimizes, the devastating
effects of evil and *poshlost*.

With metaphysical doubt absent and psychological
conflict eliminated, genuine humor, devoid of the black
or sinister overtones which one finds in *The Petty
Demon*, is allowed to prevail. We could say of these
tales what Ivanov-Razumnik remarked about Remizov's
equally charming collection of juvenilia, *Posolon*, that
"there is nothing terrible, nothing incomprehensible;
there are no tears or drama, and if there are, they are
only simple and innocent tragic-comedies."[10] Sologub's
fairy tales contain a comic, often frivolous and whimsi-
cal tone, which make them unique in his entire *oeuvre*.
"The *Book of Fairy Tales*," wrote Bryusov, "has yet another special advantage, there is laughter in it, so much
of which is lacking in the new, always too serious
art..."[11] Indeed, because of the symbolists' pervasive
sense of hopelessness, disharmony, and psychological dis-
placement, humor rarely appears in their work. But here,
where Sologub experiences a genuine *joie de vivre*, radi-
ant laughter, joyousness, and brightness occur.

The humorousness of the *skazki* results ultimately
from the writer's ability to stand outside himself and to
abandon his traditionally contemplative attitude toward
life. Of all Sologub's writing, the *Fairy Tales* are
where the authorial persona is most conspicuously absent.
As such these works may be viewed as Sologub's fullest
attempt at escape. Ordinarily concerned with his own

adult ego, obsessed with his lyrical "I," Sologub abandons his self-centered world. In this fairy-tale existence, the painful consciousness of evil is noticeably
absent because Sologub flees his metaphorical cell of
claustrophobic guilt and sin. We are at the furthest
reaches of Login's oppressive burden in *Bad Dreams* which,
as he says, increases with the passage of time. The
fairy tales present a world unencumbered by physical and
temporal concerns, a realm, like the child's, where all
is a state of continuous becoming and endless potential.
As in the case of "The Magic Wand," the past is repeatedly obliterated so that life can begin constantly anew.
Tolkien could easily have been reading Sologub's fairy
tales when he claimed about the genre that it "opens a
door on Other Time, and if we pass through, though only
for a moment, we stand outside out own time, outside
Time Itself maybe."[12] Consequently, we can claim that
only in the *Fairy Tales* does Sologub finally join the
realm of the child by, as it were, emotionally fusing
with him and, on the narrative level, becoming one himself.

     The theme of transformation, of man's need and abil-
ity to change himself and his surroundings in ways that
are infinitely diverse and exciting, runs constantly
through Sologub's writing. Ludmila often dresses Sasha
in different costumes; Elisaveta in *A Legend in Creation* loves to change into a sailor-boy's suit and herself is transformed into her other half, Queen Ortruda,
in Volume Two of the trilogy; another of Sologub's
female characters is transformed into a white dog in a
story by the same name (1908). But it is the *Fairy
Tales* where transformation reaches its apogee. Throughout the work, in the form of the narrator, the adult becomes fully and permanently what is most precious of all
to Sologub—the child himself, and all of life undergoes
a marvelous transfiguration. It is less than accidental
that the volume of stories which follows the *Fairy Tales*
in Sologub's *Collected Works* is entitled *The Book of
Transformations*.

     Sologub's life-long goal of conflict-free innocence
and purity is achieved, if anywhere, in his most fantastic works. In them the writer perceives life through the
transluscent shroud of reverie and they might just as
easily have been called "sny"—dreams. He is concerned
far less with possibility than with desirability, and
this is as it should be in fairy tales. The famous

Russian folklorist, Boris Sokolov, has defined the fairy
tale as a type of dream compensation, a vision about a magical world where nature is conquered.[13]   And Sologub's
Fairy Tales do indeed represent the highest fulfillment,
the clearest exemplification of Trirodov's credo that
"all that is beautiful in life has become real through
dream."

Sologub, then, accomplishes on the literary level
what his artist-hero will call for spiritually—the complete return to the special status of childhood. With
this comes the greater feeling of oneness with the beautiful world which the writer believes accompanies, and
truly defines, this state. Only in the works where the
child's presence predominates completely is the Sologubian ideal of enchanting transcendental otherness
reached. Of his numerous works which deal with children, it is his *Fairy Tales* which, perhaps, most fully
capture the landscape and tone of childhood. And that
the transformation, indeed the creation, of this ideal
state comes about essentially through the medium of the
child's special vision and language corroborates Trirodov's seminal idea that higher worlds can be produced
through creative fantasy and artistic imagination, that
is, through *words*. The fairy tales stand as a confirma-
tion of Trirodov's—and Sologub's—cherished belief that
art is the most beautiful means of escape and the secur-
ist refuge from the tedium of life. Art, like the fairy
tale, is pure fantasy and deception, but of a most re-
assuring kind. This is a literary credo curiously
reminiscent of another Russian master of the fantastic,
and one who in some ways is Sologub's kindred spirit,
Vladimir Nabokov. "Great novels," he has said, "are all
great fairy tales ... literature does not tell the truth
but makes it up."[14]

What Sologub's *Fairy Tales* argue and what Trirodov
openly articulates is that all of life's unavoidable
difficulties are overcome by creative vision. To be
sure, life itself can be a fairy tale, as it is for the
child, if our eyes and mind, like the child's, are
trained to perceive it as such.

NOTES

[1]Sologub's interest in fairy tales extended to the
realm of drama as well. His play *Night Dances (Nočnye
pljaski,* 1908) is called a "Dramatic Fairy Tale in Three

Acts," and is preceded by a note in which the author admits that the play's theme is inspired by the fairy tale of a similar name, found in the collection of A. N. Afanas'ev (Moscow, 1897).

[2] See in particular Roger Sale, *Fairy Tales and After* (Cambridge: Harvard University Press, 1978) and Vladimir Propp, *Morphology of the Folktale*, 2nd edition (Austin: University of Texas Press, 1968).

[3] See especially R. Jakobson, "On Russian Fairy Tales," in *Russian Fairy Tales* (New York: Pantheon, 1945), pp. 631-656.

[4] D. S. Mirsky, op. cit., p. 446.

[5] R. Jakobson, op. cit., p. 648.

[6] M. Vološin, Review "Gr. Al. Nik. Tolstoj: *Soroč'i skazki*." *Apollon*, 3 (1909), p. 23.

[7] A. Dolinin, op. cit., p. 59.

[8] V. Brjusov, op. cit., p. 50.

[9] R. Ivanov-Razumnik, op. cit., p. 72. Sologub expounds upon this notion in his article "Dèmony poètov" (*Sobranie sočinenij*, X, 169-186) where he speaks in terms of the lyrical, i.e., that which rejects the world as it is and which is directed to the realm of ideals and possibilities, and the ironic, i.e., that which accepts the world and which is directed to the given in life.

[10] R. Ivanov-Razumnik, "Aleksej Remizov," in *Tvorčestvo i kritika, 1908-1922* (Petrograd: Kolos, 1922), p. 78.

[11] V. Brjusov, op. cit., p. 51.

[12] From J. Tolkien, *Tree and Leaf*. Quoted in Sale, op. cit., p. 94.

[13] According to R. Jakobson, op. cit., p. 650.

[14] Quoted in Alfred Appel, "*Ada* Described," in *Tri-Quarterly* 17 (1970), p. 160.

CONCLUSION

More consistently than any other character, the child is linked to some of the central elements in Sologub's fiction—to the search for a different state of soul and to the related dream of creating an alternative reality. Yet the positive aspects of these elements have generally been ignored in Sologub and with them the fundamental role of children in his prose. Of course, a casual and often unrepresentative sampling of this writing, read in isolation and without regard to broader contextual and chronological position, might easily produce judgments about the author which, upon fuller consideration, prove to be misleading. This has been the problem with most criticism on Sologub in the past, particularly with regard to children.

One does tend to be struck by the darker and more bizarre aspects of Sologub's idiosyncratic world view. His works are pervaded by gloomy urban landscapes, an abundance of *poshlost*, a constant sense of alienation from his surroundings, a fascination with death and decay, and an inordinate attentiveness to erotic and sadistic, as well as other perverted behavior. Nonetheless, the philosophical fullness of Sologub's writing cannot be explained, nor can its aesthetic richness be appreciated, by an approach which views the writer exclusively as a poet of blackness. In this sense, literary criticism has dealt Sologub a grave injustice. Methodology based on such selectivity has been particularly injurious in Sologub's case, considering his penchant for contradiction and his occasional shifts in mood. For example, revealing though it is, Poggioli's analysis of the writer exemplifies this kind of approach. His emphasis solely upon negative themes implies the persistence of Sologub's renowned devil worship, when in fact such a phenomenon was a fleeting expression of only one facet of his divided personality; it was merely one of the several masks which he donned. The title of a chapter in *The Circle of Fire*, "Masks of Experiences" ("Ličiny pereživanij"), as well as of a collection of stories, *Rotting Masks (Istlevajuščie ličiny*, 1909), suggests the prevalence of the mask motif in Sologub's writing; the continual urge to change poses and moods. A systematic study of the child's connection to this phenomenon has long been overdue, particularly since Sologub consistently and quite revealingly donned the mask of the child.

Ivanov-Razumnik sensed this when he observed, using as emblematic examples the innocent and sinister boys, respectively, in "The Sting of Death," that "Kolya and Vanya are two sides of the same Sologub."[1] Admittedly, the brighter strain in Sologub's writing is often obscured and occasionally vanquished by a bleak vision, especially at the turn of the century. However, the former's sheer persistence and growing predominance will not permit us to ignore or underestimate its value in providing a fuller comprehension of the art which it informs. So acknowledged Sologub's wife, herself an enlightened commentator on her husband's writings, warning that "it would be very unfair to characterize Sologub's work as a whole as pessimistic, for besides indicating the imperfection of life and of social attitudes (*A Legend in Creation*), the poet calls for the transformation of vulgar reality via Dream and Deed."[2] Sologub's summons to transform existence came somewhat later in his career, but the escapist impulses responsible for it had been present from the very beginning. The failure of past goals and the sultry, oppressive atmosphere of the 1880s instilled in him a fierce indignation toward material life and a respect for, indeed, a dependence upon, his private world as the source of all sustenance and inspiration.

The theme of release, with its underlying desire to transcend one's current self and surroundings, has widespread philosophical implications in Sologub, but its relationship to the artistic form of his *oeuvre* should be mentioned first. It is an arresting fact that "the struggle for idealism" (recalling Volynsky's phrase) determines the fundamental pattern of Sologub's symbolist aesthetics. Symbol, myth, legend (the latter representing for Sologub the ultimate fulfillment of myth, its highest realization) signal a heuristic desire to discover in life a deeper, more positive meaning and a salvational ideal amid evidence which would tend to deny their existence. But of equal importance is the fact that these categories reflect and motivate the very structural foundations of Sologub's prose fiction. A study of the child's diverse roles suggests that Sologub's division of his narrative fiction into the modes of story, novel, and fairy tale is largely influenced by his differing perspectives on the focus of otherness: symbolic, mythical, and legendary.

Such a structural distinction becomes evident when
the particular function which the child assumes vis-à-vis
Sologub's transcendental vision is examined. In the
stories, where the child is depicted as a symbol of an
other-worldly existence, although still rooted to the
physical confines of everyday reality, the author seeks
to establish the location, and to verify the existence,
of this otherness. In the novels, where the child reflects the positive heroes' attempts to achieve or create this beautiful otherness, the child indicates Sologub's desire to believe in a myth of redemptive beauty.
Finally, in the fairy tales, where the child exists
wholly in the fantastic world of legend, Sologub most
fully allows himself to accept, and be enveloped by, the
poetry of otherness. The free, spontaneous, and joyous
existence for which Sologub continually strives is here
ultimately achieved. The important point to bear in
mind is that in each mode of Sologub's fiction, childhood indicates a yearning for timelessness. It signals
a rejection of the linear process and inevitable laws of
history in favor of a blessed state of forgetfulness or
an existence governed solely by personal will.
        That the mythic element should be connected specif-
ically with Sologub's novels is supported by Donald
Fanger's insight on Dostoevsky's art.

> (It) may be that in Tolstoy's terms, Dostoevsky
> is redeemed by his *myth*, which is based on com-
> passion and the will to believe. Here the dif-
> ference in genre comes to the fore because myth,
> as Ivanov says, requires more than symbols or
> even the vision that creates them, it requires
> action, story, pattern—such as are possible
> only in the novel, heir to the classical epic
> and drama. In this sense, although a lyric
> poet may have a system, he cannot have a myth.[3]

The chronological span of Sologub's novels, roughly
twenty years, shows that the positive heroes in each increasingly escape into the search for and creation of
beauty. It is this theme, with its repeated variations,
which constitutes Sologub's quest for myth. As this
process continues, the protagonists' involvement with
children grows accordingly. Thus, while Trirodov is
Sologub's most solitary and isolated character, he is
also the one who is most frequently involved with

children. Solitude is a prominent motif in symbolist
writing, yet in Sologub's novels it is not synonymous—
as it often is elsewhere—with inactivity. In the writer's poetry, the lyrical "I" usually prefers to withdraw
into pure solipsism as it contemplates the beauty of
death and nothingness. Such is not the case with Sologub's positive protagonists. They are not, in the final
analysis, superfluous creatures who accept passivity or
self-destruction as viable alternatives to evil and
poshlost. On the contrary, they actively struggle to
overcome life's ugliness by achieving a deed which would
verify the integrity of their individual will. The very
pattern and action here, as Fanger suggests they need to,
imply myth—in this case, the search for beauty and the
attainment of a living faith in its redemptive quality,
as Sologub understood these to exist in his favorite
novel, *Don Quixote*. Like the central figure of Cervantes' novel, Sologub's protagonists—Login, Ludmila,
Trirodov—are, in increasing intensity, dreamers. Each
is more committed than the former to realizing his personal, idealist vision of finding and creating beauty in
life.

        Sologub himself acknowledges the relationship be-
tween the child's varying functions—as symbol in the
stories—and as part of a myth, which deals with man's
need to find beauty in his life, in the novels. In "The
Art of Our Day," he notes: "In contact with various experiences [that which Ivanov calls plot and action,
S.R.] the symbol is capable of engendering from itself
myth."[4]

        Sologub would thus serve to qualify for inclusion
in Ivanov's category of the "'realist' symbolist," who
"reveals the myth in the symbol, for the myth is the objective truth of the ultimate essence of things."[5] The
critic E. Anichkov, for one, argues this. "Fedor Sologub is a characteristic mythmaker," he discovered in
1923. "His very expression 'a legend in creation' signals this. He creates myths ... and not images or allegories, because they are so clear that you cannot help
but believe in them."[6] With his reference to faith,
Anichkov rightly shifts the emphasis from the literary
to the metaphysical aspects of Sologub's myth. Indeed,
aesthetic considerations alone do not reveal the importance of the child's connection to the mythical dimension of Sologub's fiction. If one agrees with Ivanov's
supposition that "to create myth is to create belief,"[7]

then it is clear that this character's significance is
based as much on philosophical as on aesthetic grounds.
As he reveals the steady movement of Sologub's work toward legend and myth, so, too, the child reflects growing
optimism and "creation of belief."

"I want to say to you that in such moments, one does
'like dry grass,' thirst after faith.... I want to say
to you, about myself, that I am a child of this age, a
child of unfaith and skepticism ... how dreadfully it has
tortured me ... this longing for faith, which is all the
stronger for the proof I have against it."[8] Dostoevsky
confessed to his brother midway during his Siberian exile
in a statement which he could have repeated, and literarily did, at the end of his life—in *The Brothers Karamazov*. Whether Sologub ever penned similar words we do not
know, since his letters remain largely unpublished. But
if his writing in any way reflects his spiritual biography, as Dostoevsky's mirrors his, then we can be sure
that he easily might have. Certainly Ivanov-Razumnik,
who was always well-attuned to the philosophical dimensions of Sologub's writing, thought as much. As early as
1908, he insisted that the desperate search for harmony
and order in light of life's metaphysical chaos, the obsessive need to know and believe in a final purpose of
man's existence—vulgar, petty, and evil though it is—
constituted the central focus of Sologub's work. "He is
tied to (Dostoevsky) by his relationship to the Karamazovian questions which ate away at his heart with their
poison,"[9] the critic argued, and in doing so suggested an
influence on Sologub, the magnitude of which has since
been unexamined. Sologub's is not, like Dostoevsky's,
the religious faith of a zealous Christian believer, yet
in both writers a fear of life's meaninglessness continually alternates with strivings to fathom its higher goal.
"He couldn't live without his 'holy Jerusalem,'"[10]
Ivanov-Razumnik aptly put it. Although Sologub may not
have countered Ivan Karamazov's negative musings on the
meaning of life with quite the spiritual force or re-
ligiosity of a Dostoevsky, his relentless concern for a
redemptive aesthetic is nevertheless equally persistent.
Thus the child, who is the major bearer of Sologub's attempted faith in a beautiful ideal which would secure
life's ultimate justification, while not necessarily
holding an answer to the Karamazovian problems, serves
as an accurate guide to the writer's every labor at
their resolution. And it was such incessant labor which

led some readers, among whom was included the poet Maksimilian Voloshin, to rank Sologub with the giants of Russian prose. "Where has the tragedy of the Russian soul
been expressed?" he asked in 1910, "Not in the theater,
but in the novel—in Dostoevsky, Tolstoy, and Sologub."[11]

As our discussion of Sologub's children has indi-
cated, the writer's literary corpus does not reveal a
spiritual evolution which ascends in an uninterrupted
line from an oppressive despair to a comforting faith.
The fact that "Dream on the Stones" was written side-by-
side with the optimistic *Smoke and Ashes*, and that the
enchanting fairy tales were composed shortly after "The
Sting of Death" serves as ample proof of this. Yet, we
should note that this very metaphysical oscillation, often within the same work, imparts to Sologub's writing,
as it does to Dostoevsky's, its genuine sense of individual torment. Sologub's image of a devil's swing, in
his poem by the same title, ceaselessly moving man between heaven and earth "up and back" ("vpered, nazad,"
as the poet repeats again and again), appropriately characterizes the continual and torturous shifts in philosophical positions and their accompanying moods in Sologub's work at large. The sense of tormenting doubt,
which the dreary climate of the 1880s nurtured in Sologub, never prevented him from believing in the possibility of life's higher purpose; but, conversely, this
agonized wavering was rarely far beneath the surface of
his work, even during its more optimistic moments.

Yet, for all the spiritual vacillation which Sologub's prose reflects, one can detect within it sufficiently dominant states of mind to allow us to speak of
fairly distinct stages, as well as of an overall direction, in his search for a positive ideal. It is precisely the child's role which charts the rhythm of these
stages. The stories in which children play the dominant
role, and where the question of beauty's existence is
addressed, constitute three separate responses, the
chronological order of which is determined by the different answer provided in each. In Sologub's first
story "Shadows" (1894), Volodya points to a blessed insanity as a form of escape from life's "fatal contradictions," which are themselves signaled by the story's
title. In the second group of stories, published largely
between 1896 and 1898, the child is associated with an
essentially nonearthly realm of serene nature, which now
replaces madness as Sologub's alternative to disharmoni-

ous life. Finally, the third constellation of stories,
written mostly between 1899 and 1904, reflects a switch
in the focus of Sologub's dream from nature to death; for
the children here, the peaceful realm of nonbeing represents the state where beauty can best be realized.

Of course, in all of these pieces, children reflect
a common belief that the ideal can be reached only beyond
the earthly realm. Realizing the contradictions here, as
well as the writer's inability at this time to find a
lasting faith, Ivanov-Razumnik concluded that "(Sologub)
could not help but see that to answer the questions about
the meaning of life with the notion of death meant not to
answer them at all."[12] Any resolution of this dilemma
must consider the question of whether man can achieve the
higher purity and perfection which he seeks in this
world, in the here-and-now. With the adult protagonist
now in central position, the novels broach this topic,
and once again the child serves as the master symbol of
beauty, the attainment of which alone can make life
meaningful. The immediacy of the goal is matched by the
closeness of the beauty which the protagonist seeks. No
longer is the ideal embodied or sought in death or in
distant nature; rather it is epitomized in the perfection of the child himself, often in the beauty of his
naked body.

Both Login and Ludmila look to the unclothed child
as the highest embodiment of their transcendence of
poshlost'. Such an image, so persistent in Sologub and
so fraught with erotic overtones, encouraged many critics
either to exclude the writer from serious literary consideration or to concentrate largely on extra-literary
matters when dealing with him. "(Sologub's) museum-like
work stands beyond the boundary of literature and in the
majority of cases his works evoke interest mainly for
psychiatrists,"[13] Jury Steklov proclaimed in a statement
which reflected, if not in its tone then at least in its
spirit, a significant direction of contemporary Sologub
criticism. Even for those who expressed their objections
without hostility, resentment of Sologub's allegedly perverted attitude often hampered not only a full investigation of the child's role in his work, but also a serious analysis of his writing in general. The critic
Kranixfeld is a case in point.

I am deeply indebted to Sologub for the
enjoyment which several works provided -

> especially those in which children figure.
> He loves children and feels himself to be a
> master in the basic world of their naive ex-
> periences. And because he loves and under-
> stands children, I feel now not only pity but
> also indignation toward the artist who (even)
> in this, his beloved world, is unable to re-
> frain from his 'piquant - mystical experi-
> ences.'[14]

Kranixfeld's observation is correct, but limited. Bare,
sunburned limbs, long dark eyelashes and large eyes;
young boys usually between eight and fourteen who are
invariably victimized (in what L. Voytlovsky[15] calls a
cheap attempt to imitate Dostoevsky); naked bodies which
become highly eroticized objects—all of these persistent
motifs suggest, as Mirsky says, "a peculiar 'complex'
that is the result of a long-suppressed libido ...
(which) is not for the literary historian, but rather the
specifically-trained psychoanalyst to study in detail."[16]
Yet, even that which might be diagnosed as Sologub's
pedophilia retains a profound seriousness, for rarely
does this writer employ decadent themes in a purely arbitrary or exhibitionistic manner, devoid of metaphysical
significance or artistic merit. Sologub suggested as much
in his poem, "Amfora," comparing his art to a beautiful
urn which a slave balances perfectly on his shoulders to
prevent the poison within it from spilling. Poggioli's
description of Sologub's lyrics in terms of this poem,
"pure in form, even when impure in content," applies to
the prose as well. And the perspective on these "impur-
ities" which he offers in his conclusion that "(an)
ethical awareness redeems Sologub's poetry from the cheap
and vulgar immoralism which stains such a large body of
decadent writing,"[17] is appropriate to a discussion of
the image of children in the writer's fiction.

In the two novels we have mentioned the child serves
as a medium through which Login and Ludmila strive toward
a more lofty existence. Their appreciation of this character's perfect beauty or "pure form" signals their desired release from *poshlost*. However, even though "impure in content," i.e., when his characterization carries
erotic overtones, the child neither forfeits his serious
purpose in these works nor detracts from their artistic
quality. On the contrary, particularly because of their
content, Sologub's writings disclose what Vengerov has
labeled "a tragic psychology."[18] The child functions as

the barometer of Login's and Ludmila's corruptibility—
Lenya, as the object of the former's perverted homosexual
impulses, and Sasha, as the catalyst for the latter's
growing cult to sensuality. But this character is far
less important as an indicator of Sologub's alleged
pathological depravity than he is as a measure of the
writer's openness in discussing what he deemed as the
tragedy of the human pursuit of perfection. By his persistent appearance in the fiction, the child may point to
certain aberrations in Sologub's personal world, much as
he reveals the private erotic fantasies of some of the
writer's protagonists. Yet Sologub insisted that "the
intimate become the universal," and in the case of the
child, Sologub's private mythology does attain to a general scale. For in his role in the novel, the child reveals the striking contradiction between what Sologub
believes are two fundamental truths of man's personality:
his need for an absolute ideal and his seemingly uncon-
trollable urge to defile it just as it is ready to be
attained. Sologub's image of the child is complicated
by a clearly post-romantic attitude of ambiguity and
tragic irony. Throughout all of Sologub's writing runs
the longing for blessed harmony, countered as it is by
the pain over the consciousness of man's own responsibility for its loss or dissolution. The child is more than
just a symbol of this perfection; he is the very gauge of
man's unarguable distance from it.

To be sure, the otherness which the child has elsewhere shown to exist outside of life is, in *Bad Dreams*
and *The Petty Demon*, made to appear more accessible to
man. But the latter's success in approaching it still
remains in question. Such is not the case in *A Legend
in Creation*. Here the child reflects less the hero's
concern for locating the specific quality of the ideal
in a naked embodiment than his desire for a continual
reminder that beauty can be produced at will. The quiet
children, who embody various traits of beauty (gravelike
tranquility, natural purity and innocence), just as they
combine different elements of life and death, convey one
of Sologub's most mature philosophical ideas. To reduce
the ideal to any fixed characteristic is to risk being
slavishly trapped by it; to associate beauty with purely
ephemeral passion and desire is to invite inevitable
disappointment. Thus, in Sologub's later work, the
sexual and erotic overtones which characterize the hero-
child relationship, are largely eliminated. Furthermore,

Trirodov's resurrection of Egorka and his transformation
of the child into a more perfect being, demonstrate that
the higher purpose which gives meaning to man's existence
is attained by using life itself to create this state,
and not by relinquishing life and escaping into some
exalted state. It is not a case in *A Legend in Creation*
of the hero's accepting life and therefore forfeiting his
romantic visions, but, on the contrary, a question of
Trirodov's producing art and therefore rejecting his current and unacceptable fate.

The child's reflection early in Sologub's career of
a disbelief in the possibility of finding meaning and
purpose in the here-and-now yields, in the later period,
to a faith in life's ability to provide the victory over
the human condition which man seeks. In *A Legend in
Creation* Sologub discovers that faith, like creation, is
an ongoing process. Only by creating beauty—not once
and for all or in one absolute from—but continuously
and in ever-changing variations, does man constantly affirm the integrity of its existence.

That Sologub's literary children themselves reflect
in practice what the writer suggests in theory is abundantly clear. Products of a continual process of artistic creativity and ongoing changes of philosophical vision, these characters represent the most diverse contours of Sologub's fertile imagination. Their uninterrupted appearance over a twenty-year period reveals a
deep commitment to finding a meaningful order to counteract what Sologub viewed as a confusing and contradictory
reality. They also increasingly affirm a fundamental
belief that art itself can create its own reality, more
sublime and beautiful than the present one. Aware of
the great realist tradition, which was only recently
ebbing as he embarked on his literary career, Sologub
attempted to depict with an obvious lack of sympathy the
immediacies of ordinary reality. As part of the increasingly more influential symbolist generation, which
viewed literature as able to change the world, he also
created alternative visions. As such, Sologub's literary children are at the center of his most vicious pictures of reality as well as his loveliest portrayals of
dream. In each case the child shows the writer's continual fluctuation "between heaven and hell," while at all
times he bears the unique stamp of one of the most original stylists and idiosyncratic artists of the modernist
period.

Sologub's children are intimately connected with almost every turn and direction of his thought, but it is
clear that the writer was neither a great thinker nor a
profound philosopher. And it is not in this area that
his works, or the children within them, necessarily ex-
cel. "Sologub's complexity is not as much ideational as
it is emotional,"[19] Gornfeld said, stressing that the
writer's strongest impact is to be felt primarily on the
affective level. Sologub's ability to construct artistically a private mythology and to translate the innermost thoughts and feelings of his highly individualized
vision of reality into the subtle and extremely effective language of mood can be considered as the hallmark
of his literary talent. Strikingly modern, both in his
obsessive attention to his own inner world and in his
consciousness of its relentless instability, Sologub
created a suitable and elastic style to suggest the different shades of psychic atmosphere which are present at
any given time. Often, and particularly in the stories
about children, a work reflects little else besides one
of these shades. When taken together, Sologub's children
represent the most varied modes of his thought. But to
evaluate them without considering the particular tone,
mood, and emotional coloring which each helps to evoke
is to disregard the essence of Sologub's uniquely personal voice and to underestimate the artistic quality of
the prose in which it is sounded.

As much as, or perhaps more than, any other body of
writing in the Russian literary tradition, Sologub's art
is the art of self-revelation. Few writers delved as
deeply into their own personal anguish and expressed
these torments with Sologub's openness and persistence.
Each character reflects the unique stamp of the writer's
subjective world; each engages in a constant and single
dialogue with him. Unlike Chekhov, who continually
sought to conceal the author's persona, Sologub gave
vent in his work to his most fervent convictions and most
private feelings. Man's helplessness, his penchant for
self-contradiction, his pettiness, weakness, and corruptibility—themes which Chekhov treated as well—are conveyed in purely personal terms, as the confession and
revelation of the author's unmistakable "I." That Sologub so boldly disclosed the peculiarly pathological aspects which lie at the core of man's insecurity, that he
betrayed an awareness of man's own deviance as the basic
cause of his alienation and continual neurosis, proves

that he is very much a writer of our own century. Chukovsky sensed the unmistakably contemporary flavor of
Sologub's work when he insisted, as we said earlier,
that Sologub's work was a mirror which accurately reflected the modernist epic.

Having understood the supremely sensitive world of
the child, Sologub used this character as a medium to
express the broadest spectrum of responses to life. If
Sologub found it necessary to turn inward and express
artistically his deepest and most intimate emotions, then
he did so most revealingly through the fictive portrayal
of his literary children. A study of these characters,
at the very least, demonstrates that the range of feeling
in Sologub is far greater than is customarily conceded.
Sologub's style is often characterized by considerable
self-control, but whenever he does submit to emotional
surges the child is likely to be involved.

The wit and enchantment in the fairy tales and the
shame of humiliation in "The Search"; the joyousness over
nature's magic in "The Snow Maiden" and the oppressive
boredom in "Dream on the Stones"; the bitter disappointment in life's ordinariness in "The Two Gotiks" and the
awkward confusion over its ambiguities in *The Petty
Demon*; the angry offense at injustice in "The Youth
Linus" and the melancholy resignation over man's fate in
"The Worm"; the fascination with mystery in "Shadows"
and the attractiveness of nonbeing in "The Sting of
Death"—all express and personalize, by means of the
child, the interior recesses of the writer's soul. If
one agrees with Gornfeld, as Bely and Bryusov did, that
"(Sologub) is one and his work is one ... (in which) all
the experiences contained within it veer toward the center ... the center being the one, all-powerful, all-
created, all-inclusive "I" of the poet,"[20] then it is to
the very core of this center that the child points.

With the increasing investigation of the writings—
particularly the prose fiction—of Bely, Bryusov,
Remizov, and Sologub, the artistic innovativeness and
literary mastery which the age of symbolism generated
are becoming evident. The occasional "excesses" of the
period can neither obscure nor diminish the genuineness
of its aesthetic contributions or philosophical concerns.
Sologub was part of a generation of writers whose imaginations were not to be curtailed in the struggle for an
idealism which would counteract the unacceptable dismal-
ness of current reality. Mythologies were created,

visionś formulated, and utopias imagined—all in the
search for higher and better worlds. The artistic freedom which accompanied, and which was necessary for,
these strivings, yielded, predictably, talents of various
orders and qualities. Sologub's talent was itself errat-
ic, and the child reveals both the high and low points of
his literary corpus. But one would do well to recall the
words of the writer's autobiographical hero, Trirodov—
himself a litterateur, when he admits: "I write only that
which I can say myself from myself, that which has still
not been said. And there is still much which has not
been said. Better to add one's own thing than to write
volumes of trivialities" (XVIII, 197). Perhaps more than
any other of his fictional creations, Sologub's literary
children confirm that he did say his "own thing"—uniquely and with a great, if eerie, beauty.

NOTES

[1] R. Ivanov-Razumnik, op. cit., p. 33.
[2] A. N. Čebotarevskaja, "Biografičeskaja spravka," in
S. A. Vengerov, op. cit., p. 13.
[3] Donald Fanger, op. cit., p. 258.
[4] "Iskusstvo našix dnej," p. 40.
[5] G. Donchin, op. cit., p. 79. Donchin here is discussing Ivanov's article, "Dve stixii v sovremennom
simvolizme" (1905).
[6] E. Aničkov, *Novaja russkaja poèzija* (Berlin, 1923),
p. 90.
[7] V. Ivanov, *Po zvezdam*, p. 282. Quoted in J. West,
op. cit., p. 56.
[8] F. M. Dostoevskij, Letter to N. V. Fonvizin, in op.
cit., pp. 70-71.
[9] R. Ivanov-Razumnik, op. cit., p. 83.
[10] Ibid., p. 25.
[11] M. Vološin, "Imel-li xudožestvennyj teatr pravo
incenirovat' *Brat'ey Karamazovyx*? - Imel," in *Utro
Rossii*, 1910 (Oct. 22), p. 4.
[12] R. Ivanov-Razumnik, op. cit., p. 35.
[13] Jurij Steklov, "O tvorčestve Fedora Sologuba," in
Literaturnyj raspad (St. Petersburg, 1909), p. 166.
[14] V. Kranixfel'd, "Fedor Sologub," *V mire idej i
obrazov* (St. Petersburg, 1912), p. 45. Kranixfel'd's
last phrase, "pikantno-mističeskix obrazov," is an echo
of Volynskij's description of Sologub's early works. The
latter's review is not only highly unfavorable to Solo-

gub's literary productions, but also has personal implications—as did many reviews of Sologub's works—to
which the author was always extremely sensitive. Volynskij writes: "ego (vlečet) ... ne k bezdnam žizni, a k
truščobam pošlo-izmučennoj duši ... (k) pikantno-
mističeskim oščuščenijam." A Volynskij, "Novye tečnija
...," p. 238.

[15] L. Vojtlovskij's precise remark about Sologub's
alleged sadism, "Kakaja-to kucaja Dostoevščiny," is to
be found in his article, "Sumerki iskusstva," in *Literaturnyj raspad*, II (St. Petersburg, 1909), p. 50. Quoted
in G. Donchin, op. cit., p. 139.

[16] D. S. Mirskij, op. cit., p. 442.

[17] R. Poggioli, op. cit., p. 111.

[18] S. A. Vengerov, "Pobediteli ili pobeždennye?" in
Sobranie sočinenij (Petrograd, 1919), 68.

[19] A. Gornfel'd, op. cit., p. 62.

[20] A. Gornfel'd, op. cit., p. 18.

Sologub as school inspector, St. Petersburg, ca. 1905

Sologub and his wife, Anastasya Chebotarevskaya, 1908.

BIBLIOGRAPHY

Ajxenval'd, Ju. "Deti u Čexova." *Siluèty russkix pisatelej*, Vol. II. Moscow, 1917, pp. 211-226.

Aničkov, Evgenij. "Melkij bes." *O Fedore Sologube*. Ed. A. N. Čebotarevskaja. St. Petersburg: Šipovnik, 1911, pp. 217-211.

————. *Novaja russkaja poèzija*. Berlin, 1923.

Annenskij, Innokentij. "O Sologube." *O Fedore Sologube*. Ed. A. N. Čebotarevskaja. St. Petersburg: Šipovnik, 1911, pp. 217-221.

Appel, Alfred. "*Ada* Described." *Triquarterly*, 17 (1970), pp. 160-186.

Asmus, V. "Filosofia i èstetika russkogo simvolizma." *Literaturnoe nasledstvo*, No. 27-28. Moscow, 1937, 1-53.

Azov, V. "Dvenadcat' pljux." *O Fedore Sologube*. Ed. A. N. Čebotarevskaja. St. Petersburg: Šipovnik, 1911, pp. 347-350.

Barker, Murl. "Introduction." *The Kiss of the Unborn and Other Stories* by Fedor Sologub. Trans. Murl Barker. Knoxville: University of Tennessee Press, 1977, XIII-XXXVI.

————. "The Novels of Fedor Sologub." Diss. Yale, 1969.

————. "Reality and Escape: Sologub's 'The Wall and the Shadows.'" *Slavic and East European Review*, 4 (1972), pp. 419-426.

Belyj, Andrej. "Dalaj-lama iz Sapožka." *Vesy*, 3 (1908), pp. 63-76.

————. "Istlevajuščie ličiny." *O Fedore Sologube*. Ed. A. N. Čebotarevskaja. St. Petersburg: Šipovnik, 1911, pp. 96-98.

————. *Masterstvo Gogolja*. Moscow: Academia, 1934.

Bettelheim, Bruno. *The Uses of Enchantment: The Meaning and Importance of Fairy Tales*. New York: Alfred Knopf, 1976.

Bjalyj, G. "Sovremenniki." *Čexov i ego vremja*. Moscow, 1977, pp. 5-19.

Blok, Aleksandr. "O *Melkom bese*." *Sobranie sočinenij*. Vol. V. Moscow, 1962, pp. 124-129.

Boas, George. *The Cult of Childhood*. London: The Warburg Institute, 1966.

Bocjanovskij, V. "O Sologube, Nedotykomke, Gogole, Groznom, i proč." *O Fedore Sologube*. Ed. A. N.

Čebotarevskaja. St. Petersburg: Šipovnik, 1911, pp. 42-83.

Bristol, Evelyn. "Fedor Sologub's Post-Revolutionary Poetry," *American Slavic and East European Review,* 3 (1960), pp. 414-422.

_____. "The Lyric Poetry of Fedor Sologub." Diss. University of California (Berkeley), 1960.

Brjusov, Valerij. Rev. of F. Sologub. *Kniga skazok* (Moscow, 1904). *Vesy,* 11 (1904), pp. 50-52.

_____. Rev. of F. Sologub. *Sobranie sočinenij,* I. (St. Petersburg, 1910). *Russkaja mysl',* 3 (1910), pp. 53-54.

Brodsky, Patricia. "Fertile Fields and Poisoned Gardens: Sologub's Debt to Hoffmann, Pushkin, and Hawthorne." *Essays in Literature,* 1 (1974), pp. 96-108.

Čebotarevskaja, Anastasja. "Biografičeskaja spravka." *Russkaja literatura XX veka,* II. Ed. S. A. Vengerov. Moscow, 1915, pp. 9-13.

_____. "Isadora Dunkan v prozrenijax Fridrixa Nitšče." *Zolotoe runo,* 4 (1909), pp. 81-83.

_____, Ed. *O Fedore Sologube. Kritika, stat'i i zametki.* St. Petersburg: Šipovnik, 1911.

_____. Rev. of Frank Wedekind. *Probuždenie vesny* (St. Petersburg, 1907). *Russkaja mysl',* 10 (1907), pp. 195-197.

_____. "Tvorimoe tvorčestvo." *Zolotoe runo,* 10 (1908), pp. 55-68.

Cexnovicer, Orest. "Predislovie." F. Sologub. *Melkij bes.* Moscow: Academia, 1933, pp. 5-28.

Čiževskij, Dmitrij. "O platonizme v russkoj poèzii." *Mosty,* 11 (1965), pp. 198-205.

Costello, D. and Foote, I. *Russian Folk Literature.* Oxford: Oxford University Press, 1967.

Cournos, John. "Fedor Sologub." *Fortnightly Review,* 104 (1915), pp. 480-490.

_____. "Introduction." *The Old House and Other Stories.* London: Alfred Knopf, 1915, pp. 3-10.

Coveney, Peter. *Poor Monkey.* London: Rockliff, 1957.

Čukovskij, Kornej. "Nav'ji čary Melkogo besa." *O Fedore Sologube.* Ed. A. N. Čebotarevskaja. St. Petersburg: Šipovnik, 1911, pp. 35-62.

_____. "Putevoditel' po Sologubu." *Sobranie sočinenij.* Vol. VI. Moscow, 1965, pp. 332-367.

Čužak, N. "Ot Peredonova k *Tvorimoj legende.*" *O Fedore Sologube.* Ed. A. N. Čebotarevskaja. St. Petersburg: Šipovnik, 1911, pp. 222-229.

_____. "Tvorčeskoe slovo." *O Fedore Sologube*. Ed.
A. N. Čebotarevskaja. St. Petersburg: Šipovnik,
1911, pp. 238-250.
Dikman, M. "Poètičeskoe tvorčestvo Fedora Sologuba."
Fedor Sologub: Stixotvorenija. Leningrad: Sovetskij
Pisatel', 1975, pp. 5-74.
Dolinin, A. "Otrešennyj: k psixologii tvorčestva F.
Sologuba." *Zavety*, 7 (1913), 35-58.
Donchin, Georgette. *The Influence of French Symbolism
on Russian Poetry*. 'S-Gravenhage: Mouton, 1958.
Dostoevskij, Fedor. *The Brothers Karamazov*. Trans.
Constance Garnett. New York: Random House, 1958.
_____. *The Diary of a Writer*. Trans. B. Brasol.
New York: Braziller, 1954.
_____. *The Idiot*. Trans. Constance Garnett. New
York: Random House, 1942.
Džonson, I. "V mire mečty." *O Fedore Sologube*. Ed.
A. N. Čebotarevskaja. St. Petersburg: Šipovnik,
1911, pp. 120-128.
Eliade, Mircea. *The Myth of the Eternal Return*. New
York: Pantheon, 1954.
Fanger, Donald. *Dostoevsky and Romantic Realism*.
Chicago: University of Chicago Press, 1967.
Field, Andrew. "The Created Legend: Sologub's Symbolic
Universe." *Slavic and East European Journal*, 19
(1961), pp. 341-349.
_____. "Sologub's Prose: A Critical Analysis of its
Symbolism and Structure." Master's Essay, Colum-
bia, 1961.
_____. "Translator's Preface." *The Petty Demon* by
Fedor Sologub. New York: Random House, 1962,
XVII-XXII.
Foss, Martin. *Symbol and Metaphor in Human Experience*.
Lincoln: University of Nebraska Press, 1964.
Geršenzon, M. "F. Sologub: Istlevajuščie ličiny." *O
Fedore Sologube*. Ed. A. N. Čebotarevskaja. St.
Petersburg: Šipovnik, 1911, pp. 113-119.
Gibian, G. and Tjalsma, W., Eds. *Russian Modernism:
Culture and the Avant-Garde, 1900-1930*. Ithaca:
Cornell University Press, 1976.
Gippius, Zinaida. "Slezinka Peredonova." *O Fedore
Sologube*. Ed. A. N. Čebotarevskaja. St. Peters-
burg: Šipovnik, 1911, pp. 72-78.
_____. *Živye lica*. Prague: Plamja, 1925.
Gofman, Modest. *Kniga o russkix poètax poslednego
desjatiletija*. St. Petersburg, 1908.

_____. Rev. of F. Sologub, *Istlevajuščie ličiny.*
(Moscow, 1907). *Vestnik Evropy*, 7 (1907), pp. 373-
376.

Gornfel'd, A. "Fedor Sologub." *Russkaja literatura XX
veka*, II. Ed. S. A. Vengerov. Moscow, 1915, pp.
14-64.

_____. "Nedotykomka." *O Fedore Sologube.* Ed. A. N.
Čebotarevskaja. St. Petersburg: Šipovnik, 1911,
pp. 256-260.

Gorodeckij, Sergej. "Na svetlom puti." *O Fedore
Sologube.* Ed. A. N. Čebotarevskaja. St. Petersburg: Šipovnik, 1911, pp. 273-285.

Grečiškin, S. and Lavrov, A. "Andrej Belyj: Pis'ma k F.
Sologubu." *Ežegodnik rukopisnogo otdela Puškinskogo Doma*, 1972, pp. 131-137.

Gurevič, Ljubov'. "Istorija *Severnogo vestnika.
Russkaja literatura XX veka*, I. Ed. S. A. Vengerov. Moscow, 1914, pp. 235-264.

Hansson, Carola. *Fedor Sologub as a Short-Story Writer:
Stylistic Analyses.* Stockholm: Almquist and
Wiksell, 1975.

Holthusen, Johannes. *Fedor Sologubs Roman-Trilogie:
Tvorimaja Legenda.* The Hague: Mouton, 1960.

_____. "Sologubs Satirisch-Utopische Trilogie."
Tvorimaja Legenda von F. Sologub. Munich: Fink
Verlag, 1972, i - xii.

Il'jin, V. "Fedor Sologub - 'Nedobryj' i zagodočnyj."
Vozroždenie, 15 (1957), pp. 58-75.

Ivanov, Vjačeslav. *Freedom and the Tragic Life.* New
York: Noonday, 1960.

_____. *Po zvedam.* St. Petersburg: Grif, 1909.

Ivanov-Razumnik, R. "Aleksej Remizov." *Tvorčestvo i
Kritika: 1908-1922.* Petrograd: Kolos, 1922, pp.
57-82.

_____. "Fedor Sologub." *O Fedore Sologube.* Ed. A. N.
Čebotarevskaja. St. Petersburg: Šipovnik, 1911, pp.
7-34.

_____. *O smysle žizni'.* St. Petersburg: Stasjulevič,
1908.

_____. *Pisatel'skie sud'by.* New York:Literaturnyj
fond, 1951.

Ivask, Jurij. "Fedor Sologub: K sorokaletiju so dnja
smerti: 1927-1967." *Russkaja mysl'*, No. 2664,
Dec. 7, 1967, n.p.

Izmajlov, Alexksandr. "Čarovanija krasnyx vymyslov." *O

Fedore Sologube. Ed. A. N. Čebotarevskaja. St.
Petersburg: Šipovnik, 1911, pp. 296-305.
_____. "Izmel'čavskij krasnyx vymyslov." *O Fedore
Sologube.* Ed. A. N. Čebotarevskaja. St. Peters-
burg: Šipovnik, 1911, pp. 286-295.
_____. "Severnyj sfinks." *O Fedore Sologube.* Ed.
A. N. Čebotarevskaja. St. Petersburg: Šipovnik,
1911, pp. 261-272.
Jackson, Robert. *Dostoevsky's Quest for Form.* New
Haven: Yale University Press, 1966.
Jakobson, Roman. "On Russian Fairy Tales." *Russian
Fairy Tales.* New York: Pantheon, 1945, pp. 631-651.
Jampol'skij, I. "F. Sologub: Pisma k L. Ja. Gurevič i
A. L. Volynskomu." *Ežegodnik rukopisnogo otdela
Puškinskogo Doma,* 1972, pp. 112-130.
Kalbous, George. "The Plays of Fjodor Sologub." Diss.
New York University, 1970.
Kaye, A. Lister. "Sologub." *Fortnightly Review,* 108
(1920), pp. 663-671.
Kogan, Pavel. *Očerki po istorii novejšej russkoj liter-
atury,* III. Moscow, 1910.
Kranixfel'd, Vladimir. "Fedor Sologub." *V mire idej i
obrazov.* St. Petersburg, 1912, pp. 3-45.
Krasnov, P. "Russkie dekadenty." *Trud,* 11 (1895), pp.
449-460.
Levin, Harry. *James Joyce.* New York:New Directions,
1960.
Lossky, N. *A History of Russian Philosophy.* New York:
International Universities Press, 1951.
Maguire, Robert. "Macrocosm or Microcosm" The Symbol-
ists on Russia." *Russia: The Spirit of Nationalism.*
New York: St. Johns University Press, 1972, pp.
125-152.
Malmstad, John. *Mixail Kuzmin: A Chronicle of His Life
and Times.* M. A. Kuzmin: Sobranie Stixov III.
Munich: Wilhelm Fink Verlag, 1977, pp. 15-313.
Maslenikov, Oleg. *The FrenziedPoets.* Berkeley: Univer-
sity of California Press, 1951.
Mašbac - Verov, I. *Russkij simvolizm i put' Aleksandra
Bloka.* Kujbyšev, 1969.
Mirsky, D. Ș. *A History of Russian Literature.* New
York: Alfred Knopf, 1958.
Mochulsky, Konstantin. *Dostoevsky: His Life and Work.*
Trans. M. Minihan. Princeton: Princeton University
Press, 1967.
Muchnic, Helen. *Russian Writers: Notes and Essays.*

174   Bibliography

New York: Random House, 1971.
Muratova, K. D. *Istorija russkoj literatury konca XIX -
načala XX veka. Bibliografičeskij ukazatel'.*
Moscow, 1963.
New Jerusalem Bible. New York: Doubleday, 1966.
Novopolin, G. *Pornografičeskij èlement v russkoj liter-
ature.* St. Petersburg, 1909.
Poggioli, Renato. *The Poets of Russia.* Cambridge: Har-
vard University Press, 1960.
Propp, V. *Morphology of the Folktale.* Second ed.
Trans. Laurence Scott. Austin: University of
Texas Press, 1968.
Rabinowitz, Stanley. "Bely and Sologub: Toward the His-
tory of a Friendship." *Andrey Bely: A Critical
Review.* Ed. G. Janacek. Lexington, Kentucky: Uni-
versity of Kentucky Press, pp. 156-168.
_____. "Fedor Sologub and His Nineteenth-Century Rus-
sian Antecedents." *Slavic and East European Jour-
nal,* 3 (1978), pp. 324-335.
_____. "On the Death of a Poet: The Final Days of
Fedor Sologub." *Russian Literature Triquarterly,*
15 (1978), pp. 360-368.
_____. "Sologub's Literary Children: The Special Case
of *Melkii bes.*" *Canadian Slavonic Papers,* 4
(1979), pp. 503-519.
Red'ko, A. "Ešče problema." *Russkoe bogatstvo,* 1
(1910), pp. 130-144.
_____. "F. Sologub v bytovyx proizvedenijax i
v'tvorimyx legendax'." *Russkoe bogatstvo,* 3 (1909),
pp. 55-90.
_____. "Obrazcy krasoty čelovečeskoj." *Russkoe
bogatstvo,* 12 (1912), pp. 347-364.
Reeve, F. D. "Art as Solution: Sologub's Devil," *Modern
Fiction Studies,* 3 (1957), pp. 110-118.
_____. *The Russian Novel.* New York: McGraw Hill,
1966.
Ronen, Omry. "Toponyms of F. Sologub's *Tvorimaja
legenda.*" *Die Welt der Slaven,* 13 (1968), pp. 307-
316.
Rosenthal, Bernice. "Nietzsche in Russia: The Case of
Merezhkovsky." *Slavic Review,* 3 (1974), pp. 429-
452.
Rowe, William. *Dostoevsky: Child and Man in His Works.*
New York: New York University Press, 1968.
Rozenfel'd, A. "F. Sologub." *O Fedore Sologube.* Ed.
A. N. Čebotarevskaja. St. Petersburg: Šipovnik,

1911, pp. 208-216.

Ryss, Petr. *Portrèty*. Paris, 1924.

Sale, Roger. *Fairy Tales and After*. Cambridge: Harvard University Press, 1978.

Selegen', Galina. *Prexitraja vjaz'*. Washington: Victor Kamkin, 1968.

Simmons, Ernest. "Introduction." *The Petty Demon* by Fedor Sologub. New York: Random House, 1962, VII-XV.

Slonim, Marc. *From Chekhov to the Revolution*. New York: Oxford University Press, 1962.

Smith, Vassar. "*On Bad Dreams.*" *Russian Literature Tri-Quarterly*, 16 (1979), pp. 86-91.

Sokolov, Yu. *Russian Folklore*. Trans. Ruth Smith. Hatboro, Pa.: Folklore Associates, 1966.

Sologub, Fedor. *A Legend in Creation*. Trans. Sam Cioran. Ann Arbor, 1979, 3 vols.

_____. *The Kiss of the Unborn and Other Stories*. Trans. Murl Barker. Knoxville: University of Tennessee Press, 1977.

_____. "Ljubov' i smert'." *Birževye vedemosti*, 24, February, 1917, p. 6.

_____. *Melkij bes*. Ed. O. Cexnovicer. Moscow: Academia, 1933. (Bradda Reprint, 1966.)

_____. *The Old House and Other Stories*. Trans. John Cournos. New York: Alfred Knopf, 1916.

_____. "O grjaduščem xame Merežkovskogo." *Zolotoe runo*, 4 (1906), pp. 102-104.

_____. *The Petty Demon*. Trans. Andrew Field. New York: Random House, 1962.

_____. *Plamennyj krug*. Berlin: Gžebin, 1922.

_____. *Sobranie sočinenij*. 20 Vols. St. Petersburg: Sirin, 1913-1914.

_____. *The Sweet-Scented Name and Other Fairy Tales, Fables and Stories*. Ed. Stephen Graham. New York: Putnam's and Sons, 1915.

Spasskij, Ju. "Nav'ji čary." *O Fedore Sologube*. Ed. A. N. Čebotarevskaja. St. Petersburg: Šipovnik, 1911, pp. 319-324.

Steklov, Jurij. "O tvorčestve Fedora Sologuba." *Literaturnyj raspad*, II (1909), pp. 319-324.

Stromberg, Roland. Ed. *Realism, Naturalism, and Symbolism*. New York: Harper and Row, 1968.

Struve, Gleb. "Tri sud'by: III. Rycar' pečal'nogo obraza." *Novyj žurnal*, XVIII (1947), pp. 204-211.

Thurston, G. "Sologub's *Melkij bes*." *Slavic and East European Review*, 1 (1977), pp. 30-44.

Tindall, William. *The Literary Symbol.* Bloomington:
    Indiana University Press, 1965.
Tolstoj, Lev. *Detstvo, Otročestvo, Junost'.* *Sobranie*
    sočinenij, Vol. I. Moscow, 1960.
_____. *Vojna i mir.* Moscow, 1957.
Ul'janovskaja, B. "O prototipax romana F. Sologuba.
    Melkij bes." *Russkaja literatura,* 3 (1969), 181-
    184.
Vengerov, S. A. "Pobediteli ili pobeždennye?: O russkom
    modernizme." *Sobranie sočinenij,* Vol. I, Petrograd,
    1919, pp. 46-79.
Vergežskij, A. "Tjaželye sny." *O Fedore Sologube.* Ed.
    A. N. Čebotarevskaja. St. Petersburg: Šipovnik,
    1911, pp. 342-346.
Vladimirov, P. "Fedor Sologub i ego roman *Melkij bes."*
    O Fedore Sologube. Ed. A. N. Čebotarevskaja. St.
    Petersburg: Šipovnik, 1911, pp. 306-318.
Vološin, Maksimilian. Rev. A. N. Tolstoj. *Soroč'i*
    skazki. Moscow, 1909. *Apollon,* 3 (1909), pp. 23-
    24.
Volynskij, A. *Bor'ba za idealizm.* St. Petersburg, 1900.
_____. "Novye tečenija v sovremennoj literature -
    Fedor Sologub." *Severnyj vestnik,* 12 (1896), pp.
    235-246.
West, James. *Russian Symbolism.* London: Metheun, 1970.
Xodasevič, Vladislav. "Sologub." *Sovremennye zapiski,*
    XXXIV (1928), pp. 347-362.
Zakrževskij, Aleksandr. "Fedor Sologub." *Podpol'e:*
    Psixologičeskie paralleli. Kiev, 1911, pp. 29-54.
Zamjatin, Evgenij. *Lica.* New York:Chekhov Publishing
    House, 1955.
Žirmunskij, V. "On Rhythmic Prose." *To Honor Roman*
    Jakobson: Essays on the Occasion of His Seventieth
    Birthday. The Hague: Mouton, 1967, pp. 2376-2388.

OTHER BOOKS FROM SLAVICA PUBLISHERS

Alexander Lipson: *A Russian Course*, xiv + 612 p., 1977.

Thomas F. Magner, ed.: *Slavic Linguistics and Language Teaching*, x + 309 p., 1976.

Meteja Matejić & Dragan Milivojevic: *An Anthology of Medieval Serbian Literature in English*, 205 p., 1978.

Vasa D. Mihailovich and Mateja Matejić: *Yugoslav Literature in English A Bibliography of Translations and Criticism(1821-1975)*, ix + 328 p., 1976.

Alexander D. Nakhimovsky and Richard L. Leed: *Advanced Russian*, xvi + 380 p., 1980.

Felix J. Oinas, ed.: *Folklore Nationalism & Politics*, 190 p., 1977.

Hongor Oulanoff: *The Prose Fiction of Veniamin A. Kaverin*, v + 203 p., 1976.

Jan L. Perkowski: *Vampires of the Slavs* (a collection of readings), 294 p., 1976.

Lester A. Rice: *Hungarian Morphological Irregularities*, 80 p., 1970.

Midhat Ridjanovic: *A Synchronic Study of Verbal Aspect in English and Serbo-Croatian*, ix + 147 p., 1976.

David F. Robinson: *Lithuanian Reverse Dictionary*, ix + 209 p., 1976.

Don K. Rowney & G. Edward Orchard, eds.: *Russian and Slavic History*, viii + 311 p., 1977.

Ernest A. Scatton: *Bulgarian Phonology*, 224 p., 1975.

William R. Schmalstieg: *Introduction to Old Church Slavic*, 290 p., 1976.

Michael Shapiro: *Aspects of Russian Morphology. A Semiotic Investigation*, 62 p., 1969.

Rudolph M. Susel, ed.: *Papers in Slovene Studies, 1977*, 127 p., 1978.

Charles E. Townsend: *Russian Word-Formation, corrected reprint*, xviii + 272 p., 1975 (1980).